HOPE IN CAPTIVITY

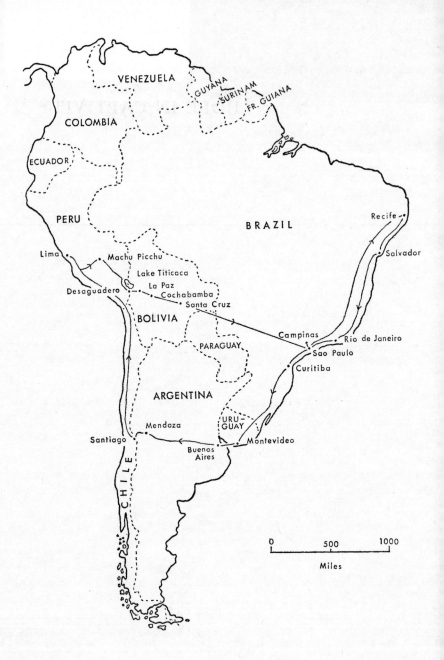

Derek Winter

HOPE
IN
CAPTIVITY

*The Prophetic Church
in Latin America*

London
EPWORTH PRESS

7162 0283 2

Enquiries should be addressed to
The Methodist Publishing House
Wellington Road
Wimbledon
London SW19 8EU
Printed in Great Britain by
The Garden City Press Limited
Letchworth, Hertfordshire SG6 1JS

To the memory of
BERYL
beloved wife
and fellow-worker
in Brazil

ACKNOWLEDGEMENTS

In most instances, notes following the text show
the sources from which quotations from
copyright work have been made by permission
of the publishers concerned, but additionally
grateful acknowledgement is due for the excerpt
on p. 114 from *The Alternative Future; A Vision
of Christian Marxism*, by Roger Garaudy © 1976,
reprinted by permission of Penguin Books Ltd;
the excerpt on p. 124 from 'An Open Letter to
José Miguez Bonino', by Jurgen Moltmann,
reprinted from 29 March 1976 issue of
Christianity and Crisis © 1976, reprinted by
by permission of Christianity and Crisis Inc.;
the excerpts on pp. 73-4, 99, 119-23 from
LatinAmerica Press, Apartado 5594, Lima 1, Peru;
the excerpt on p. 94 from *Practical Theology of
Liberation*, by Hugo Assmann © 1975,
reprinted by permission of Search Press; and to
the *Baptist Times* for permission to use material
on pp. 49-52 and pp. 88-92 which appeared in
articles in that journal in February and April 1976.

CONTENTS

Inspiration from Latin America

THIS IS the fascinating story of a former missionary who returns to the places of his earlier ministry and finds out that he had missed an important part of reality during his mission there. He had preached the text of the Bible but missed seeing the Brazilian reality, the all-important context of his text. He had overlooked the context which puts the biblical story into focus and helps us to discover its liberating message.

Before going back to Latin America, Derek Winter had had to earn the money for his journey by working on the night shift in a British factory—a good preparation for a man who wants to discover the hopes and aspirations of people at the grass-roots. His research was originally intended for an academic dissertation. However, the university requirements for the writing of a dissertation seemed to him to conflict with the needs of the people for whom he wished to write, the people that matter to him, the ordinary Christians in Great Britain. He decided to write for *these* people and to forget about the thesis. I regret this decision. Does it mean, I ask myself, that the rules of a British university prevent a man from writing understandably and relevantly for the whole people of God? Or does it mean that we have not yet developed forms of academic research which are both academically accurate and helpfully relevant for the majority of the people—those who support the university by their taxes?

One part of his story in particular has stuck with me for many days. I cannot forget the testimony of Helmut Frenz, Bishop of the German Lutherans in Chile and courageous defender of the prisoners of the Pinochet regime. 'I once asked my parents', Frenz told Derek Winter, 'why they didn't react to the persecution of the Jews. "We didn't know", they replied; but they didn't know because they didn't want to know.'

I found myself thinking a lot about that question. What are the questions our children will ask us? Perhaps they will ask: Is it true that in the late seventies there was a civil war in Northern Ireland? Is it true that one of the richest, most ingenious and most privileged nations in the world had to borrow billions just in order to finance its huge and overblown administration, in order to keep alive industries which were obviously out-dated, over-manned, ill-equipped and badly managed, in the hope of creating sometime in the distant future a new and viable economic and industrial order? Is it true that the British people didn't want to know that they were rapidly becoming a country of the Third World, not because of brutal outside interference and reckless internal colonialism like the Latin American countries, but because of the incompetence and complacency of their own management, trade union leaders and politicians? Is it true that the British government time and time again forecast a recovery which never material-ized and yet still went on making further blatantly unrealistic statements? When they ask these questions, will we say to our children, 'We didn't know', and will they answer, 'You didn't want to know'? They will go on to ask: Is it true that this state of the nation was constantly discussed not in the context of reality—that context in which the Bible becomes a liberating book, a context in which there is the possibility of repentance and a new beginning—but within the polarization model of left-wing and right-wing politics, as if nationalization or denationalization, Socialist or Tory rhetoric, an elitist or a populist bureaucracy would make the slightest difference to the obvious deficiencies of labour relations and production processes? Is it true that some of the most thoughtful people abandoned their right to vote because it no longer mattered to them whether they were bamboozled by this or the other party, whether shallow compromises and inadequate services were 'explained' by one or the other propaganda liturgy, whether the stop-go policy of their leaders was covered up by one or the other ideology? Is it true that leading politicians told the British people that if the government were to do what they should there would be riots in the streets because many people were not prepared to face reality?

Fortunately I have no children. But that does not prevent my being asked these questions by the younger generation, both here in Great Britain and in my own home country. The painful fact of the matter is that I cannot answer, 'I didn't know.' I know enough to see the outcome of the disastrous pettiness of both ecclesiastical and political leaders, their kind ignorance, their gentle cowardice and their hypocritical search for scapegoats at home and abroad.

Derek Winter describes the paralysis which grips the Latin American people over against foreign intervention and the spiritual revival of some of the Christians who try courageously to do theology on the basis of reality, thus demonstrating realistic long-term options. But what do we do if our plight cannot be blamed on foreigners, if it is the result of our own inadequacies, of our own dream-world politics? Well, I think John the Baptist would invite us to take a long, hard look at ourselves and to come to term with ourselves. The New Testament calls this repentance.

Repentance is different from gloominess and pessimism. Repentance carries with it the promise of forgiveness and a new beginning. How can I, as a missionary to this country, help myself and British Christians to do theology in the context of this promise? I cannot answer this question, nor will it be answered by Derek Winter's book. He shows us an example of people who are certainly in a more difficult situation than we are. Yet their hope in captivity, their prophetic ministry enables them to do theology in the context of reality, on the issues which matter and with the people who matter. We have the same God, believe in the same biblical message. They have hope because they face reality—so why can't we?

WALTER J. HOLLENWEGER
Professor of Mission
University of Birmingham

Birmingham
January 1977

PREFACE

THIS book arises from a Latin American journey undertaken during a period of study leave from St Paul's College, Cheltenham. I should like to record my thanks to the Principal and Governors of the College for the opportunity thus offered.

My further debt of gratitude to a large number of friends, old and new, who were lavish with time, conversation and hospitality, will be evident to any reader of this book—a debt far too great to record in detail. But I cannot fail to express my thanks to my former BMS colleagues in Brazil, who while disagreeing with me on many matters were prepared to engage in friendly dialogue; to Professor Walter Hollenweger of Birmingham University, for his constant encouragement and criticism; to Miss Brenda Kemeys, who reduced the chaos of my manuscript to typewritten order; and to my daughter Janet, who in the midst of A level work cheerfully accepted the responsibility of running the home during my three-month absence in the spring of last year.

DEREK WINTER

Cheltenham
Advent 1976

In seminaries and universities we are used to the idea of considering theology as an academic discipline, as a degree programme in the liberal arts. The historical fact is that once upon a time theologising was a very different sort of activity, a dangerous one in fact. It certainly was not a 'liberal art' for men like the prophets and Jesus. They died before their time because of their theologising, because of their specific way of interpreting the word of God and its implications for the liberation of the oppressed ... only academic theologians can talk about the 'death of God'. In the concrete struggle for liberation, the danger is not the death of God but the death of the theologian.

J. L. Segundo

INTRODUCTION

THE pages that follow are just one man's view of the prophetic church in Latin American—a view both partial and partisan. Partial, because on my journey I visited only six countries out of twenty (although these six contain about two-thirds of the population south of the Rio Grande); and partisan, because I deliberately sought out people who in some way or other are consciously doing theology and living their faith in the context of the struggle for liberation. The people introduced in these pages are representative of this growing minority which transcends denominational barriers, for it is a fellowship of people drawn together by a common response to human need and by a common rediscovery of the revolutionary meaning of the gospel.

For many years, I myself belonged to the church of the silent majority who consciously or unconsciously accept the social, economic and political *status quo* in Latin America. From 1957 to 1970 I was a Baptist missionary in Brazil. I worked within the context of the Brazilian Baptist Convention, doing pastoral and educational work in the developing and progressive state of Paraná. And my lack of awareness of the political implications of the faith I tried to share is sufficiently illustrated by an incident I recorded in a letter from Brazil in April 1964, the year when the present military government seized power.[1]

I was visiting two brothers, members of the local Baptist church, who worked a small holding they had cleared of forest and planted with cereal crops, near the North West Paraná town of Goioerê. José and his brother had quarrelled bitterly with some relatives, who had threatened to kill them; so they had gone to the local police to ask for protection. But when

17

they showed up at the police station, they were promptly put behind bars on a charge of being communists.

'Apparently', I wrote, 'José's brother-in-law had taken advantage of the anti-communist witch-hunt that swept the country after President Goulart's downfall to denounce them, saying that they had openly preached communism and harboured communist literature. Of course, it was a fantastic charge. The tiny grain of truth behind it was that two years ago, in self-defence against the injustice of a land-owner on whose farm they used to work, they had signed on as members of the rural workers' trade union, which was communist-led. When the right wing *coup d'état* took place a month ago, this organization was proscribed and its leaders put in jail—those of them who did not run for it in time, like the Goioerê branch secretary. But hundreds of rural workers who had signed on have been questioned by the police, and some of them jailed until their homes could be searched or their innocence of communist sympathies otherwise proved. When the police were satisfied that the charge against the Sampaio brothers could not be substantiated—the only subversive literature found in their shack was the Bible!—they were released.'

The reference to the Bible is, of course, facetious. It is partly because I have since discovered how subversive the Bible really is that this book was written.[2]

It is not primarily a book for those already familiar with the growing volume of Latin American theology of liberation available in English, although I hope that the attempt to describe some of these theologians against the background of their local situation may help to illuminate their thought, and to explain the diversity of their distinctive contribution. (To some extent it is misleading to speak at all about Latin American theology of liberation as if it were a monolithic system.) I have, rather, borne in mind those who are interested in the role and function of the church in Latin America, whether they have been used to thinking of her peoples as the most devoutly Catholic folk anywhere in the world, or whether they have been intrigued by the reports of the spontaneous expansion of the Protestant (and especially the Pentecostal) churches. Either way, they cannot fail to be aware of another dimension to the reality of the Latin American church—the growing conflict between church and state over the question of social justice and human rights. This is a very recent phenomenon, and, given the history of the church in the sub-continent, it has taken governments by surprise.

The basic facts and broad outline of the history of Christian faith in Latin America are well known. 'Christianity entered Latin America under two historic movements: conquest and colonization in the sixteenth century and modernization and neo-colonialism in the nineteenth.'³ The Spanish conquistadores of the Aztec and Inca civilizations, the Portuguese explorers who sailed with Pedro Alvares Cabral to the coast of Brazil in 1500, taking possession of the land in the name of the King of Portugal—all these brought with them to the new world the Catholic faith; not only so, they inevitably imported the relation between the Catholic church and the Hispanic class structure, in which the church paid for its patronage by the small group of landowning families with the coin of complete subservience to the ruling class. 'The colonial church was tied to a colonial structure.'⁴ Thus a sacral society was set up in the new world, not so different in concept from the sacral societies of China, Egypt and Babylon which had flourished 2,000 years before. God in his heaven, the king of Spain on his throne, the landlord in his 'Casa Grande', this prevailing world view was legitimized by a monolithic religion. When the eighteenth-century shock waves of the American War of Independence and the French Revolution began to be registered on seismographs in South America, setting off a chain reaction of social and political upheaval, there was little doubt which side the church would be on: 'As one of the best precepts of our religion is that which enjoins submission to superior authorities, we do not doubt that in the riots that are taking place in those countries, you will not have ceased to inspire your flock with the firm and righteous hatred which they must feel toward them'—so the Pope to the Latin American bishops 150 years ago.[5]

It was not therefore surprising that in the period of modernization which followed the winning of independence from Spain and Portugal, political emancipation should go hand in hand with the demand for religious freedom, and that men should turn to Protestantism as an alternative. This expression of Christian faith came to Latin America not simply as a direct result of North American and (later) European missionary enterprise, but also through German, Dutch and other European immigrant groups. The rapid growth of the Protestant churches in Latin America within the past fifty years, especially the Pentecostal churches, is one of the best known and documented facts of twentieth-century Christianity.

Protestants were prepared to be iconoclastic towards the sacral society. Their God was the God of freedom, culture, democracy, progress—and capitalism. The social ethic of the protestant missionaries of North America could be well summed up in the true story told by a friend of mine in Brazil. He happened to be riding in the car of an American missionary when a ragged Brazilian at the roadside thumbed a lift. Without even slowing down, the American drove on, but as he did so, he threw from the car window a copy of John's gospel. My friend reacted critically to this, but the American's reply was to the effect that if the man bothered to read the gospel and was converted, before long he'd be making good and have a car of his own to ride around in!

A caricature? Perhaps, but sufficiently close to the truth to be recognizable. To be sure, by embracing a Protestant expression of Christian faith, many individuals have found a new dynamic which has enabled them to improve their standard of living and achieve a more genuinely human way of life. Further, the Protestant churches have a creditable record in the field of social concern, as the schools, colleges and hospitals they built bear ample witness. But the observation that Bonino makes of the Western missionary enterprise as a whole is all too apt in the case of Latin America: 'The result is quite often middle-class churches founded by people concerned with their individualistic (spiritual and social) promotion, having lost their solidarity with their nation and the class from which they arose, uncritically supporting the reactionary ideology of their (real or imagined) social class.'[6] And to make matters worse, it is precisely this social class which is beginning to resemble most closely the consumer society of the North Atlantic nations, and which most benefits from the economic, cultural and military control exercised by the United States over its own 'backyard'.

This domination is maintained to a great extent through the military dictatorships which control eight of the countries south of Panama,[7] and which (with the possible exception of Peru) adopt capitalist economic policies supported by a right-wing ideology of 'national security', which claims an absolute authority for the state against the individual, and admits no political opposition in anything but name. These policies, while raising the standard of living for a minority of the population, condemn some 70 per cent of the people to a bare subsistence level in a world where illiteracy, malnutrition and appalling housing conditions are on the increase. In 1969, in his 'Report on the Americas', Nelson Rockefeller declared, 'The gap between the advantaged and disadvantaged, within nations as well as between nations, is ever sharper and more difficult to endure'. Seven years later, living conditions have become yet more intolerable.

The Latin American military dictatorships, besides clamping down on political opposition, have to a large extent succeeded in suppressing trade unions, controlling universities, and muzzling the news media. The one institution that is still capable of raising its voice in protest is the church. And the gradual transformation of a church from its role as supporter of the *status quo* to one of opposition and protest is one of the most significant facts of the contemporary Latin American scene. It is a process which is far from complete or comprehensive, as the following pages suggest; but where the process of transformation is most developed, the contribution of Latin

21

American theology of liberation is most clearly evident. If this book provides for some readers a grass-roots glimpse[8] of the prophetic church in Latin America, or encourages others to read such writers as Bonino, Gutierrez and Segundo for themselves, it will have served a useful purpose. For I do not regard this movement as a mere passing fashion in theology. The questions it raises may well set the agenda for the church— and not just in Latin America—for the remainder of this century.

CHAPTER ONE

Peruvian Revolutionaries

> To discover how religion moves from hapless cry to
> effective protest, from opiate to stimulant, is a matter
> of great urgency.
>
> *Harvey Cox*[1]

THE Ileutian 62 of Aeroflot was full of Russians and other
East Europeans on their way to the UNIDO conference in Lima.
The tall, well-built Russian air hostesses made a striking
contrast with the dark, petite Portuguese stewardesses who
shepherded us to our orange squash in the lounge at Lisbon,
which we reached in a torrential downpour. Another eleven
hours and we emerged into the tropical heat of Havana, where
the lush vegetation and friendly volatile people crowding the
airport engulfed me in a Latin American *abraço*. I was back.

Twenty-three hours out of Frankfurt we were flying down
the Peruvian coastline, the Andes visible in the distance rising
mysteriously out of the heat haze. From Lima airport, I
shared a taxi with two German medical students, Birke and
Bernhard, who had decided to give studies a break in favour
of tourism on a shoe-string. The first hotel we tried could only
offer a room with three beds, and I was almost won over by
Birke's disarming lack of inhibition—they wouldn't mind if I
didn't! But I told her that I had too much reading to do and
the light might disturb them. Eventually we found rooms in
separate places in down-town Lima, although it was eloquent
testimony to the hostelry they found that the next day they
moved to mine. For the princely sum of 80p a night I was
offered a *habitación* in the incredibly sleazy Hotel Pacifico, a
left-over from the colonial period, complete with rickety
wooden balcony hanging over the street. But you could have a
cold shower under a dripping tap, and the loo worked. The
room's previous occupant had evidently found himself

involuntarily sharing his *habitación* with other residents, for he had pencilled on the peeling plaster: 'Watch out for rats —suspend food.' It seemed incongruous that just across the road was the Peruvian equivalent of Buckingham Palace, the great courtyard of which gives on to the nearby Plaza de Armas. Here you could see twice daily the changing of the guard—dark-skinned soldiers in gold helmets, white and scarlet uniforms and black riding boots, doing a slow motion goose-step, and looking rather like two columns of friendly king penguins waddling along, except for the bayonets held at the ready.

That evening, Birke and Bernhard and I met again to discuss Latin American theology of liberation over some cigars acquired in Havana that seemed worthy of Guevara himself. Bernhard reckoned Che was becoming a cult figure to the point of unthinking religious devotion, and he may well be right. Pictures of him are everywhere, from large wall photos in smart apartments, to barely recognizable daubs on lorry mudguards. But clearly governments take the phenomenon more seriously.

Peru is one of the few places in Latin America outside Cuba where you can display pictures of Che without inviting instant arrest, and this is consistent with the leftist stance of the Peruvian military junta, which aspires to be revolutionary. Compared with most Latin American governments, it is, if expropriation of American oil interests and land reform are indications of revolutionary politics. A major-general of the Peruvian army who gave me a lift in his car waxed enthusiastic about the current move for agrarian reform, due according to government sources to be completed by June 1976. The forty traditional land-owning families were at last handing over to co-operatives. The government is also attempting to put through a far-reaching programme of educational reform, and trying to enlist popular participation in the process. But any populist movement not initiated and controlled from above is firmly discouraged by the government, which is inevitably written off by the left as paternalistic and bourgeois reformist.

Certainly, whatever reforms are put through are unlikely to improve things for the large peasant population in the remote Andean villages, whose natural economy is withering under the impact of capitalism, as local production of clothes and tools gives way to the flood of mass-produced articles from industry on the coast. 'The government doesn't give a damn what happens to these people', remarked an economics student doing research in the sierra; 'they're unimportant economically. Besides, the Peruvian generals are all coastal people. They don't know the sierra—it's another world.'

But now the world of the sierra has come to them, as many peasants, forced out of their traditional trades, or finding that agriculture on the *altiplano* can no longer support them, leave the sierra and stream down to the coastal cities to swell the ranks of the unemployment. Lima gives the impression of a city bursting at the seams. Everywhere you are surrounded by a seething mass of Peruvian humanity, with a much higher proportion of Indian features than you see in an average Brazilian crowd. Many of the women are distractingly pretty. Walking through the Parque Universitario, you're thronged by people sampling the wares of fruit stalls piled with pears, mangoes, avocados, grapes and oranges. Improvized street kitchens abound, and for 10p you can have a plateful of corn, liver and tripe fried in oil and garlic, or if you prefer, sample ceviche, fish pickled in a fantastically peppery brine. A group gathers round a Quechua woman, brown bowler hat perched on her pig-tailed hair, multi-coloured shawl and voluminous skirts, eloquently hawking copies of a book of folk remedies; at the centre of another, a wizened little man sings a repetitive ditty to the strumming of an exiguous mandolin. Down-town Lima is full of street vendors of both sexes and all ages offering trinkets, clothing, pictures—anything from paper models of Popeye to oil paintings of Machu Picchu—pathetically trying to compete in a capitalist world, and at night retiring to the indescribably squalid barriadas that encircle the city—Lima's time bomb, as one man ominously described it. For many, this means a ride in one of the villainous buses, 90 per cent of which should have been on the scrap heap twenty years ago. In the rush hour they are jammed solid, the conductor unrealistically urging people already in immediate danger of asphyxiation to move up, as he risks his life by a toe-hold in the swirling traffic. Hemmed in and hardly able to move a muscle, you look down to meet the wondering gaze of an Indian baby, eyes like little black buttons, staring up from the sling on his mother's back.

The bus ride from Lima to Rimac, one of the poorer suburbs of the city, is mercifully short. If you go to the end of the line, you find yourself on the slopes of a hill up which the shanty town sprawls, over-spilling from Rimac itself. One of the best views of these slums is afforded from the flat roof of an unremarkable three-storey building in the centre of Rimac, where Gustavo Gutierrez lives.

Gutierrez is a short, stockily built man with broad *mestizo* features, who talks volubly and with great nervous energy. He walks with a pronounced limp, the legacy of a bone disease which he contracted at the age of twelve. For six years, when most youngsters of his age would be at school, he had to stay in bed, and it was during this period that he began his studies in Humanities. When he was nineteen, he entered San Marcos University in Lima to study medicine, and at the same time began his studies in philosophy at the Catholic University. He still had plans to become a psychiatrist when four years later he left Peru to study psychology at Louvain University in Belgium. Here he met Camilo Torres. Camilo, later to achieve fame as the revolutionary priest who was killed in a guerrilla action in Colombia in 1966, and Gustavo, today a leading exponent of Latin American theology of liberation, became firm friends. 'He arrived in Louvain in '53, when I'd already been there two years', Gustavo reminisces. 'We were the same age, although he was already a priest and I a *seminarista*. He was an unassuming man, without an overpowering personality, but very lively, very open, and basically very straightforward. It was Camilo who taught me to drink wine', he added with a grin.

Gustavo then went to Lyons to study theology for four years, but on his return to Latin America in 1960 he resumed contact with Camilo, and from time to time during the next five years they worked together, teaching in seminars on sociology and theology. But Gutierrez rejects the suggestion that his social concern stems from his Louvain period or his association with Camilo—it has its roots in his student days in Lima, when he played an active part in Socialist politics. And for the past fifteen years, his chief work as a priest has been as adviser to student/worker groups. To earn his living, he teaches theology at the Catholic University; but his contacts with people in the barriadas are as strong as with university students, and it is from his involvement in Catholic groups dedicated to social action that his book *Teologia de la Liberación* has emerged. Was he surprised that it had been translated into five languages and published in so many countries? 'Yes, indeed, because I was thinking of a reader-ship in Peru and in a few other groups in Latin America.' It says much for its potentially explosive quality that it was violently attacked in an article published in Chile's leading newspaper *El Mercurio* in May—but in spite of this, some copies were still to be had under the counter in Santiago, while in Brazil the new Portuguese translation was freely available in bookshops in Rio, São Paulo and Curitiba.

Why had it become a theological best-seller? Was it, as Gustavo claimed, a new way of doing theology? Or was he simply using new terminology for old concepts that were only now being rediscovered? 'Well', he replied, 'I'd say first that what one is after in theological work isn't necessarily something new, but something useful for the life of the Christian com-munity. And maybe the first new thing is that this theology seems useful. Originality isn't something you seek—you find it. But there's something important in the desire that theology should be useful, and this is something I *do* seek. Speaking from this perspective, I said very hesitantly (and I confess that this is a phrase I crossed out several times in the manuscript, because it seemed pretentious, but in the end, on the advice of friends, I left it in) that perhaps we are on the brink of a new way of doing theology. However, if there *is* something new, it's the intention of taking praxis as the clear point of departure. You can always find precedents, as with any important idea; if anyone states it clearly, you can always say—this has been said before. But if it wasn't stated with clarity, it doesn't seem that it was said before. Here's a comparison which isn't a good one, because my work is more modest than the case I'm discussing, but I recall an instance from another field of thought, a discussion between Freud and Pierre Janet, a French psychologist. When Freud began writing his material on psychoanalysis in 1893, Pierre Janet, who had written a book in 1889, said—when psychoanalysis was already being developed—'these are ideas that I have written about before". And Freud replied: "The person who achieves something is the one who realizes what he has found—not the one who just finds it, but the one who knows how to make use of it." So I believe that praxis as the point of reference is a principle that goes a long way back—for example, in the English writer Duns Scotus, who said that God is the object of practical knowledge, not of theoretical knowledge. This is a tradition we can trace through the "practical reason" of Kant, through Marx, and so on. If this theology has something of a distinctive flavour, it is this new way of seeing the theory/praxis nexus. This for me is central.

'But perhaps the most important thing about this theology is that people who read it say, yes, this is something for me. Whether it's a question of terminology . . . well, it may be, but at least it's relevant. In Latin America, theology hasn't been discussed since the sixteenth century, the time of Bartolomé de las Casas. But more recently in Latin America theology is giving rise to controversy—there are some people who write articles saying that it's no longer theology . . . but at least it's creating interest!'

So at least it seemed to José Maria Arguedas, the Peruvian novelist whom Gustavo had come to know personally during the last year of his life and to whom he dedicated his book.

Gustavo spoke of him with affection. 'He was an Indian, a man who felt keenly the culture shock between indigenous and Western tradition. His work had a peculiarly national flavour. He died in December 1969, but a year before, when he was in Chimbote working on his last novel, a friend lent him the text of a talk of mine on theology of liberation—the first outline I wrote in July '68. When he had read it he asked this friend to introduce us. So one day we had a meal together, and he said that the paper had greatly impressed him; that he had always considered himself an atheist—but not in relation to the God of whom I had written. For him, this was something new, a new world, and he hadn't read anything with such attention and interest since he read the works of Lenin forty years ago. Hearing Arguedas say this impressed me—I felt and still feel very small compared to him. Then he read to me some of the text of his book *Todas las Sangres*—which I quoted in my book—and said: "I think I have said in my book what you are saying, that there's one God of the oppressed and another of the oppressors; as the sacristan says to the priest: 'The God of the bosses isn't the same as the God in whom I believe" '; and Arguedas added: "Now that I've read your paper, I understand better what I have written. In my heart, I always believed in this liberating God, but I didn't know him." '

This solidarity with the poor is a key feature of Gutierrez's thought. He traces the Biblical concept of poverty, from the literal meaning of material deprivation, to the spiritual concept of 'poverty of spirit'. Poverty as deprivation is, in the Bible, invariably seen as a scandalous condition, an offence abhorrent to God. Poverty contradicts the meaning of the Exodus, which was a liberation from exploitation and injustice; it contradicts the mandate of Genesis, where man is set the task of transforming nature and through his work realizing his creative freedom, whereas the poverty that has its roots in exploited labour implies work that alienates man instead of fulfilling him; and finally, poverty is an offence to God, since man is the sacrament of God who is present in the poor and

29

needy. 'To oppress the poor is to offend God himself; to know God is to work justice among men.'[2] Hence the real, material poverty of deprivation and misery can never be exalted into a Christian ideal. Just as Christ, though rich, 'became poor, so that through his poverty you might become rich', so the concept of Christian poverty must mean solidarity with the poor and a protest against poverty: 'It is a poverty which means taking on the sinful condition of man to liberate him from sin and all its consequences.'[3]

Gutierrez rejects any dichotomy between redemption from sin and liberation from the social expressions of sin, just as he rejects the dualism of 'sacred history' and secular history. His three-fold definition of liberation embraces (1) 'the aspirations of oppressed peoples and social classes' to be free from exploitation and injustice; (2) the creative historical process through which mankind gradually realizes its true humanity; and (3) the redemption by Christ from sin 'which is the ultimate root of all disruption of friendship and of all injustice and oppression.[4] Only by holding together these aspects of a single complex process can we avoid on the one hand a false spiritualization that is blind to the harsh realities of the world, and on the other, 'shallow analyses and programmes of short term effect' which may meet immediate needs but which fail to tackle the deep rooted problems of man in society.

In the same way, there are not two histories, one sacred and the other profane. 'Rather, there is only one human destiny, irreversibly assumed by Christ, the Lord of history.' And in an eloquent passage, he counters those who see liberation theology as an expression of the 'social gospel' which attenuates the real meaning of Christian faith. 'Nothing is outside the pale of the action of Christ and the gift of the Spirit. This gives human history its profound unity. Those who reduce the work of salvation are indeed those who limit it to the strictly religious sphere, and are not aware of the universality of the process. It is those who think that the work of Christ touches the social order in which we live only indirectly or tangentially, and not in its roots and basic structure. It is those who in order to protect salvation (or to protect their interests) lift salvation from the midst of history, where men and social classes struggle to liberate themselves from the slavery and oppression to which other men and social classes have subjected them. It is those who refuse to see that the salvation of Christ is a radical liberation from all misery, all despoliation, all alienation. It is those who by trying to "save" the work of Christ will "lose" it.'[5]

This understanding of the Gospel inevitably raises questions about the role of the church in Latin America, and our very way of presenting the Gospel. 'It is evident that only a break with the unjust social order and a frank commitment to a new society can make the message of love which the Christian community bears credible to Latin Americans. These demands should lead the Church to a profound revision of its manner of preaching the Word and of living and celebrating its faith.[6] Nor is this simply the pious hope of a theologian who sees that changes need to be made but is at a loss to say how; it is an expression of the changes that are already taking place. Theology of liberation is theology evolved in the context of the struggle for liberation. It is, as Miguez Bonino puts it, 'the reflection about facts and experiences which have already evoked a response from Christians.'[7] To learn something more about these facts and experiences, I went to some of the barriadas where priests associated with Gutierrez are working.

Padre Vicente's parish is at Lurim, 30 km out of town. After a forty-five-minute journey, I emerged from the battered wreck of a bus, and walked along the dusty street towards the church. All around were signs of the earthquake the previous October. Walls were being rebuilt, temporary roofs of tarpaulin and plastic had been rigged up. The church itself was a wreck. I lunched with Vicente and Padre Miguel, another Spanish priest. He had been in Spain in September '73 when Allende was overthrown, and had witnessed the return of a dozen Spanish priests who had been involved in the 'Christians for Socialism' movement, and who had been tortured before being expelled from Chile. He and Vicente are both activists who, while supporting the general line of liberation theology, reckon that each man must discover its relevance within his own particular situation. After a brief siesta in the tree-shaded patio of their home, Vicente took me to a distant part of his parish. The meeting he had arranged took place in the courtyard of the home of one of his parishioners—a concrete floor, brick walls and rush matting for a roof. I thought, I've been here before, though 2,000 miles away in Brazil. Men with faces like worn leather, women with children at the breast, toddlers sprawled on a tarpaulin, a dog scratching his fleas, scraggy chickens picking their way nervously through the yard. A dark-eyed, brown-skinned, chubby little three-year-old called Maria climbed on to my lap clutching a half-eaten apple, and within a couple of minutes, overcome by the afternoon heat, was fast asleep. My *déjà vu* sensation deepened when Padre Vicente began the meeting with choruses. But these were spiritual songs with a difference—not pious, but with a strong element of protest. The reading was from Exodus—the escape from oppression in Egypt. Questions followed. Did the same kind of injustice exist today? And was this sinful, against God's will? What were the specific injustices of our situation? That we lived in a shanty town without water, light, adequate transport, while others had all these services provided? What of rising prices and the struggle to feed a family on a pittance? What could ordinary people do about it? The least we could do was to organize ourselves with committees from other barriadas to form a pressure group and lobby the rich and powerful in trade and government. A small beginning, maybe, but it was making a start somewhere. Already there was a promise of water—an artesian well, a water tower, and pipes to be laid in the main streets—an improvement on the present system of carting water in trucks and pouring it into the barrels outside people's shacks.

On the way back, we stopped and talked with some of the people. Vicente had been there twelve years, and is well known and liked. We stepped into one man's home, the living room bare apart from a chair, table and a battered old sewing machine. He was tailoring trousers for school children. How much apiece? About £1.50. 'Sometimes I sell them cheaper to really needy folk.' He himself had ten children, and walked barefoot.

In contrast to Lurim, Vila Maria is part of Lima—a slum by the banks of the river Rimac, crowded with the most squalid hovels you'll see anywhere on earth. The priest in charge of the parish, Peter Hughes, an Irishman of the Colomban order, seems to exemplify the dictum of Gutierrez, 'that poverty ought to be embraced not to exalt it into an ideal for living, but to bear witness to the evil that it represents'.[8]

He told me about his work and the role of the church in Vila Maria. Many of these urban slums grew up around cities like Lima in the 'sixties. This happened to coincide with the 'development decade' inspired by Kennedy's vision of the Alliance for Progress, and a large number of American technicians, agronomists, doctors and priests learned Spanish and travelled south. How far all this was coldly thought out by 'the boys in Washington' as a way of maintaining imperialist influence in Latin America is debatable,[9] but there could be no doubt about the sincerity and goodwill of many of the American priests who came to work in these poor parishes. They soon discovered that it was no good dispensing spiritual values remote from the appalling conditions to be seen outside the door at every minute of the day. Parishes became channels of help in the form of food and clothing. But as a new awareness of the causes of deprivation was born, there came a new understanding of the function of a local priest. 'I see my role as an educator', he said. 'Fundamentally I'm here because I believe in a Jesus who saves, who is stronger than the misery, more powerful than the forces of evil—conscious or unconscious—that produce a situation like this.' This demands a Christian presence amid the work of political groups of the left, weak and immature as they may be, but which are at least making an honest effort to interpret the historical project of the poor, whether of Vila Maria, of Lima, of Peru, or of the whole continent. Education in this context means 'trying to awaken people, encouraging them to reflect on their situation, trying to evoke from their lives and the facts of everyday experience an understanding of the Christian God'.

In his laconic, unemotional way, Peter went on to recount an incident that illustrates his understanding of his ministry and his response to the human need around him. 'About ten days ago, something happened in this barrio that has occurred a number of times in the last few years. At this time of year the volume of water in the Rimac increases tremendously, and there's a very steep drop from the edge of the road to the river. Because there's no garbage collection service, people throw rubbish into the river, and accidents have happened. People have fallen over the brink, kids have drowned—the tragic things that happen in a barrio like this. At six one evening about ten days ago, a man came: "Padre, will you please come to the wake. My father has fallen into the river—we fished him out near Callao." When I arrived, the house was full of people—migrants from the sierra—who expected a priest to do the traditional thing at a vigil. So I tried to say something, to sympathize; but I realized I was probably the only person present who saw the tremendous injustice and limitations of people's lives in this situation, and their apparent impotence to change it. So at that moment I had two alternatives. Talk about God in a pious way, and the people will be happy, because it's their experience of God—the God they bring from the Andes with them. It's the God of patience, of resignation to one's lot, the God who makes rivers run vicious, who controls the rain and drought, with its consequences in harvest or famine; the God of fear, the God who judges, and who has to be placated.

'But I tried to do something different. This accident happened because of two things: there is no protective wall beside the road, and the lorries do not come from the municipality of Lima to collect the garbage. Because of this, people's lives end in tragedy. What God wants is that we live a more human life, without this constant danger. Maybe what God wants is that someone should build a wall there. Besides, why is it that in some parts of Lima people aren't exposed to these hazards, while the folk of Vila Maria are? What's it all about?

'I stayed the night. Two days later, on Sunday, we talked about the incident during mass. We follow two main lines. First, denunciation[10] of the situation as it is; we bear witness that living like this in despair and misery is to be denounced, both humanly speaking, and even more, in the light of a Christ who liberates. But always we start from something specific, in this case the man's death in the river. The second element of the liturgy is annunciation: we announce something better in the context of the kingdom—of the Christ incarnate, born into this world. The fact of Christ is present, but not revealed. And an acceptance of the Christian message means action, becoming aware of a new life and hope, of a task where we strive to build a better world with a sense of human rights and dignity, and an appreciation of the most humble person, a world in which there's justice not simply for the more able, lucid and strong, but justice within reach of the lowest people.

'So after mass on Sunday, a group of about twenty young people sat round, and said: "We want to do something about this. What can we do?" They kicked the ball around for about half an hour; many things were mentioned. "We have to get the newspapers here, get the incident reported in the press." Other people said: "They won't come. We're poor people, they're not interested in us. And it's pointless going to the authorities. Many times before the older people of the barrio have gone to the authorities, but because we're poor and unproductive for them, we won't get anywhere." There was an older man present, and he said, very gently, that the older people should be involved in this too. They might be tired and open to criticism, but they should be approached.

'So during all that week, the barrio got into a state of mobilization. First the young people brought out leaflets to say what happened and why it happened. A document was drawn up which was to be sent to the municipal authorities and to four national newspapers. It was done carefully, with the participation of the people and with promptings from me and Raul on certain points. But we are careful not to go before the people. When the document was drawn up, the young people approached as many families as possible in the market place and by going from house to house. People who could, read the document, and those who couldn't had it explained to them. They were not simply asked to sign on the dotted line, but were approached and asked to think a little. So two days later I met the young people and asked: "How is the work going?"—"We got a tremendous reception from the older people", they said. (This was a step forward, since the youngsters here are very critical about the older folk and their ability and will to get involved.)

'Towards the end of the week, the time came to approach the newspapers. Here I must say I accompanied them. It would have been better if they had gone alone; but then one must judge when one has to be in some way present. You could be too much on the side-lines as well. So we went to four newspapers—*La Prensa*, *Crónica*, *Correio* and *Expresso*. Right there and then the photographer came from *La Crónica*. He took photographs of the scene of the accident, talked with the people, and went away.'

It would be comfortably reassuring to be able to finish Peter's narrative with a sensational success story of how the newspapers' headlines caused a change of heart at City Hall, and the garbage collection service was inaugurated and the wall built the following week. In fact, not one word appeared in print. But an unexpected spin-off from the incident was that when the adults of the barrio came to consider the problem of rebuilding the school razed by last year's earthquake, encouraged by the social involvement of the youngsters, they decided to enlist their help. Nor is there the slightest doubt that as the process of awareness building goes on, and mutual confidence is built up within the community, concrete results will follow.

This episode and the situation it mirrors inevitably raises questions about the relation of theology of liberation and

'religiosidad popular'—or, as Gutierrez and his research colleague Raul Vidales would prefer to express it, the 'religious
practice of the exploited classes'. They both attach great
importance to the role of popular religion in sharpening and
redefining liberation theology. At their Bartolomé de las Casas
study centre in Rimac, one of their four current research projects aims at delineating more clearly the beliefs and attitudes
of the Peruvian masses. On the one hand, they are not uncritical of popular religion, avoiding what they call a populist
attitude which accepts that everything that emanates from the
people *must* be good; they recognize all that there is of an
oppressive ideology in 'religiosidad popular'. But on the other,
they see in this very religiosity a great potential. 'We want to
gather up what there is of a liberating theology in this popular
religion, to look to the people themselves as creators of this
theology, to help workers and peasants to see themselves as
agents of liberation.' How best this latent power can be discovered and harnessed, how far the evangelism practised by
the church is aiding this process, how far the religious element
is becoming an active one within the revolutionary process—
these are some of the questions that the research project aims
to investigate, with a view to the politicization and mobilization
of the people. It is, as Vidales frankly admits, a 'militant'
investigation, not an academic survey conducted from an
office, but carried out by a team of researchers who themselves
are activists working with groups in the barrios and villages.
Questionnaire are adapted to the conditions of the various
areas where the surveys are made—among the slum-dwellers
of Lima, the Andean peasants of Piura, the industrial workers
of Chimbote. The questions are detailed and pointed: What
do you think of the statement that we're all equal before God?
Why do you think there's inequality (rich and poor) between
men? Do you think God is content with this situation of
inequality? What do you consider the most pressing problems
of this barrio? Do you belong to a religious group? What
work ought such a group to be doing? Which priest do you
know best? What do you think of his work in the parish? Do

you think the people ought to unite to promote campaigns?
For what ends? This is a small sample of the mass of questions. The results should provide an interesting profile of
popular attitudes and beliefs.

A second area of research is the historical one. Vidales aptly
remarks that the Gospel has not just become a liberating force.
Time and again in history its revolutionary power has been
discovered. So a study is under way of the religious factor
within the struggles of rural workers in Latin America, and
the religious ingredient in the fight for national independence.
Even when people have not possessed a clear political awareness, the religious element has moved them in an impressive
way towards social change. One of the focal points of this
study is that of Las Casas himself, born 500 years ago, and
from whom the study centre gets its name. Las Casas was one
of the first great missionaries. Not only did he attempt to
ensure fair treatment for the Indians against Spanish exploitation, he knew how to interpret the Christian message in a way
relevant to the indigenous population. How, knowing so little
about the Indians, did he succeed in understanding and meeting their needs? It is one of the tragedies of history that Las
Casas was paid so little heed by his fellow countrymen. But
as Miguez Bonino observes, 'Men like him and others are the
fountainhead of a small but never interrupted stream of
prophetic protest in Latin American Christianity.'[11]

Increasingly, this element of protest is beginning to characterize Latin American Christianity. You read it in the books
of the theologians; you see it in the activities of the priests;
perhaps most significant of all, you hear it in the songs of the
people.

> One day I asked my grandfather:
> 'Grandfather, where is God?'
> He looked at me sadly
> but never said a word.
> My grandfather died in the fields
> without a priest or a doctor,

and the Indians buried him
playing bamboo flutes and drums.

Later I asked my father:
'Father, what do you know of God?'
My father became very serious
but never said a word,
My father died in the mines
without a priest or a doctor.
The gold of the mine-owner
is coloured with miner's blood.

My brother lives in the hills
and he never sees a flower;
only sweat, malaria, and snakes
are the life of a woodcutter.
Let no one ask him
if he knows where God is!
Such an important gentleman
has not passed near his house.

I sing along the roads
and when I find myself in gaol
I hear the voices of the people
and they sing better than I;
there is something on earth
that is more important than God:
that no one should spit blood
just to let others live better.

They say God cares for the poor.
Well, this may be true or not,
but it's the mine-owner he dines with,
and that I do know for a fact.

CHAPTER TWO

Bolivian Peasants

> As long as the blood flows in our veins, we will make
> heard the piercing cry of the exploited.
>
> *Nestor Paz*[1]

I T was during Las Casas' missionary activity in the New
World that Atahualpa, head of the Inca Empire, was executed
on the order of Pizarro at Cajamarca in 1533. At once, the
400-year-old empire disintegrated. But the Spaniards never
discovered the last citadel of the Incas, and it took nearly
another 400 years before Hiram Bingham, an American
archaeologist, stumbled upon Machu Picchu in 1911. If you're
travelling overland from Lima to La Paz, this marvellous relic
of Inca civilization is practically *en route*, just a few hours'
train journey from Cuzco.

I caught the Cuzco bus from Lima on a route which the
South American handbook optimistically tells you takes 17
hours—or was it a misprint for 70? The first leg to Nazca is
south along the Panamerican Highway. The road from Lima
leads out through the barriadas and into desert country as
arid as anything in Arizona or the Sahara. At dusk, we catch
a last glimpse of the Pacific as we turn inland to Nazca. Here
the first snag occurs. We are due to change buses, but the one
from Cuzco is late. The night is warm, and I wander the
darkened streets, or converse with some of the passengers.
Reuben is a student who has worked with a government-
sponsored scheme of literacy among the Quechua people, ex-
perimenting with Paulo Freire methods,[2] but he was dis-
appointed at the lack of response from the Indians, whom he
found shuttered and suspicious. He and his sister, Nancy, are
friendly and open, as is the teacher from Cuzco with whom I
share a front seat, in spite of my initial *faux pas* in addressing
her as señora instead of señorita—señoritas come a good deal

older in Peru than in Brazil, and I'd better not forget it!
Equally, being called gringo or gringito, usually quite without
malice, is something new—it's rarely heard in Brazil. After a
six-hour delay, we change buses and the luggage is heaved out
of the boot and on to the roof of the second bus. A couple
of protesting hens are firmly shoved back into a battered card-
board box, and we're off again.

After an uneasy couple of hours' sleep, I wake to find the
bus stopped. It's a misty morning in the Andean foothills,
and a wheel is being changed, the driver coaxing the dud
wheel off with a large wayside rock. We climb higher along a
series of hairpin bends, the dirt road hugging the mountain
with nothing between it and a 2,000-foot drop. At each bend,
if you happen to be in the front seat, you swing out over the
abyss—nothing like it for concentrating the mind. The sign
of the cross my companion made as she started the journey
is reflected in the wayside crosses that appear at frequent
intervals where someone misjudged the curve. Now I know
why no less than four saints' pictures are displayed at the
front of the bus, each with a little votive light—glowing red
foci of supplication as the bus lurches on up the sierra.

Twenty-four hours out of Lima, and fifteen thousand feet
up, I'm cold and shivery, and the meal I had at a Lima street
kitchen is playing internal havoc. A search of Puquio, the first
pueblo since Nazca which we reach in a leaden downpour,
produces nothing but a closed chemist's—it's siesta. The
baggage is transferred and we change buses yet again. As we
move on the rain clears, and as barren rock gives way to
sparse vegetation we cross range upon awesome range of the
sierra, the summits white against deep blue. The thin haze of
green is enough to support a few mangy cows, sheep and
goats, and I catch a first glimpse of a flock of llamas. The
occasional peasant, in brown poncho, scurries along the trail,
bent almost double under his load. We spend the second night
dozing in the bus outside an inn in a tiny pueblo between
Puquio and Chalhuanca, and I'm cold and running a tempera-
ture. As dawn breaks, the burly Quechua who owns the inn

41

stirs and puts me out of my misery with some herb tea, which works like a charm. But over the next leg of the journey I soon get the point of the overnight stop, for up on the altiplano the rain has ruined the track and made it hazardous even in daylight. A dozen times we pile out to lighten the load, and at one spot where water is pouring across the trail we're stuck fast for an hour, taking turns to dig under the wheels. Peru has at least one thing in common with Brazil. At last, with the help of a truck towing from behind, and everyone pushing like mad in front, the ten-ton cork shoots from the bottle and we build a causeway of boulders through the sea of mud before the driver is prepared to renegotiate that particular stretch. Soon we're descending, the road running alongside a torrent that would defeat the most skilful slalom canoeist. We cross several bridges, all of them worthy of the original 'Bridge of San Luis Rey', which a thoughtful friend with an odd sense of humour had given me to read on the trip. At one point a bulldozer is clearing a rockfall from the road. We disembark and wait. Half a mile further down, the road has disappeared altogether, and we scramble over piles of boulders while the bus makes an unloaded ascent of a tortuous track torn from the hillside further up. We finally make Chalhuanca at 4 p.m., where I gingerly sip a bowl of hot vegetable soup before reconnoitring the main square and splashing out on a bright blanket, armoury against another night in the Andes. Past Abancay the bus claws its way up into the sierra again, as we doze fitfully under the brilliant stars. By daybreak we're descending to another river, but the rain has washed away part of the approach to the bridge, and the bus sticks on the very brink. With a great display of manoeuvring skill the driver gets us off the hook, and we pause at the other bank in a flurry of tooth brushes, soap and excursions to the forest. By the time we reach bread and coffee at the next inn, we're in a wide green valley where maize and potatoes do well, and nasturtium, lupin and broom flower profusely at the wayside. Past the police check-point at the brow of the next hill, and we're looking down on the red roofs and old colonial churches of the ancient Inca capital of Cuzco. From here, it's fifty miles to Machu Picchu.

This legendary Inca fortress is almost a national symbol of Peru, and pictures of it are seen everywhere. But no photograph, nor any verbal description, can do justice to Machu Picchu. Like G. K. Chesterton fumbling for words adequate for Micawber, you walk round and round it wondering what you will say. But as you lie on one of the grassy terraces overlooking this city built on the saddle of a mountain 6,000 feet up, itself dwarfed by jagged peaks lost in the mists where condors circle, the unearthly atmosphere of the place speaks so powerfully that words themselves lose their currency. One detail, however, cannot escape comment. The stone conduits, beautifully tooled out of the rock, still bring the cool, clear water from the heights splashing into the fountains in the citadel as efficiently as they did 500 years ago. The Incas had their priorities right. Today, their descendants live herded in city slums, often without even a fresh water supply. That Andean paradise ruined and abandoned in the wake of Spanish plunder and the thirst for gold seems a symbol of Latin America in a far deeper sense than the popular tourist image of Machu Picchu—it stands for the despoliation and ruin of a whole people under the impact of colonialism.

One can travel from Cuzco to Puno by train—a day's journey through the desolate altiplano, with snow-covered peaks on the horizon. From time to time we pass large herds of cattle, sheep and llamas. Small pueblos, built of mud huts roofed with tin or rushes, can be seen from the train, and groups of peasant women in pigtails and bowler hats sit hunched together talking and spinning. The occasional beggars at wayside halts are the most pitiful members of the human race I've ever seen.

After a night's rest in Puno, I arranged to share a minibus with Klaus, a German architect touring Latin America with his wife and two teenage boys, and two Australians, Roy and Robyn. We took the dirt road that runs along the south-west shore of Lake Titicaca, the sun was shining, and the landscape less forbidding, with crops of potatoes and wheat everywhere. At one point, on the outskirts of a small town, we were held up to let by a convoy of Peruvian army trucks on manoeuvre —a sign that we were approaching the Bolivian border. Shortly after noon we reached the frontier post at Desaguadero, and typically the passport office was closed for siesta. I couldn't help feeling annoyed at Klaus' repeated expressions of contempt for these people's way of life. This is Latin America. What on earth did he expect—Teutonic efficiency?

At least, all formalities completed, we crossed over, to discover that there was another three hours before the bus left for La Paz. Apart from the seven gringos, the vehicle was crammed with Aymara women who had crossed into Peru to buy textiles at the Desaguadero street market, and smuggle them back into Bolivia. In spite of no less than three checkpoints between the border and La Paz, many a sheet and towel reaches the Bolivian capital under cover of voluminous shawls and skirts. At one customs post a woman suckled her baby to avoid being disturbed by the official. A female customs officer angrily ordered another woman off the bus to be searched, but as she protestingly descended backwards she neatly flipped a packet into my lap. I wasn't wildly enthusiastic about landing up in a Bolivian jail for the sake of a smuggled sheet, but her companion sitting behind me promptly retrieved it and hid it in her ample bosom while her friend shammed injured innocence with the official outside. At last, these entertaining charades over, we were on the move again, and by 8 p.m. we had crested a hill on the vast plateau to glimpse a blaze of myriad lights in the dramatic gorge below us. We had arrived at La Paz.

One of the people I was anxious to meet in the Bolivian capital was the Director of the Rural Research and Development Centre (CIPCA), Fr Javier Albo, SJ. Albo is a tall man with wide, open features and a penetrating gaze, his bald pate amply compensated for by a luxuriant beard. He first came from Spain to Bolivia twenty-three years ago, and has become an expert in the language and culture of the Aymara people.

When his work for the campesinos of the altiplano featured in a recent BBC TV documentary, the *Radio Times* described him as a disciple of Paulo Freire, the Brazilian educational philosopher whose radical ideas for the 'conscientization' of illiterate peasants led to his expulsion by the Brazilian military government. Did Albo accept the description?

'Not without a good deal of modification', he replied. 'In CIPCA, we do make use of Paulo Freire's methods, but we go beyond them. Conscientization, making people aware of their problems, is something that is very important and necessary; but this is only one of the factors we consider important. The second would be the social dimension of this, or mobilization. The third is economic power, without which neither of the other two factors is strong enough to change and dynamize the peasant groups. So we insist on generating economic power that is really controlled by the peasant groups themselves—and in this sense it's very different from many so-called development programmes.'

A main difference between Albo and Freire is that he considers this type of work more important than literacy. 'Literacy may be a necessary tool—but in our work the peasants are discovering their problems through many other methods besides literacy. The literacy problem will be solved through other means—through the multiplication of rural schools, through men enlisting for military service, and so on. We consider it our job to tackle their more urgent problems, regardless of whether they can read and write.'

One important means of encouraging community discussion of peasant life is the Radio Programme which CIPCA broadcasts from La Paz for two or three hours each day. One slot on the programme features a typical Aymara community called Panquar marka, an 'Archers'-type serial which mirrors life on the altiplano and provides a forum for discussing peasant values and problems. Albo provokes a lively response from campesinos scattered over a wide area, some of whom make the journey to La Paz to talk on the radio themselves and ventilate their problems. Progress towards solutions may be slow; the macro-structure is almost impossible to change ('we'd have to go to England for that!'); but at least CIPCA is making a dent on the local structure. Albo's efforts are directed to undermining what he calls the vertical links—the peasants' subservience to the city, their dependence on the merchants and officials—and to building a more horizontal structure in which co-operation between the peasant communities themselves is developed.

For example: 'Let's say they need to raise the money for a community project—perhaps a school, this is a typical thing, although it isn't the most relevant factor for change—the problem is what is taught in the school! Now, given this vertical structure, the easiest thing for them is to form a committee and come to one of the many government agencies and beg for some materials to build the school. They will offer the labour, and expect the government to provide the materials. It's easy to sell themselves to the government—to make a pact with the military, accepting the latter's nominee as leader of the peasants, provided the materials are forthcoming. This policy is successful in the sense that they will get the school; but it's the easy way out. It means they'll get constant supervision from above, and not achieve the self-sufficiency which is the only way to free them.

'What we are attempting is to convince them that they can take the initiative, that they can put aside part of their money for these materials, and where they need government help, to claim this as adults, not to beg as children—there is a difference!'

This kind of problem is related to how the campesinos sell their produce. This is often done piecemeal, through the personal 'compadre' relationship that a peasant may have with a dealer. Albo is trying to encourage co-operatives, and the selling of produce on a more organized basis. At Murumamani, the community worked together to build an experimental underground silo to store the potato crop. This enabled them to hang on to their produce until it could command a much better market price, and eliminated the profits of middlemen. Another project, first pioneered in the Corpa district of Ingavi province, provides units of twenty-five laying hens to individual families. Not a form of production traditionally favoured on the altiplano, aviculture is now spreading among a number of communities.

As a priest, Albo occasionally says Mass, but the bulk of his time is spent between the office in La Paz (which he maintains with the help of Oxfam) and the scattered pueblos of the plateau. For him, this work is the practical expression of theology of liberation. Sometimes he finds that his understanding of the Gospel brings him into conflict with the sector of his church that prefers to toe the government line of 'the church in the sacristy'; a recent government-sponsored TV programme had featured a bitter attack on Catholic radicals by six priests who had been briefed by the president himself. But Christians in touch with the needs of the deprived were not confined to the Catholics, as the outspoken 'Manifesto to the Nation' of the Methodist church clearly demonstrated. Here too, church leaders concerned with the socio-political implications of Christian faith become the targets of criticism from fellow Christians, notably Pentecostals and others associated with the charismatic movement, which for some had become a refuge from the harsh realities of government reaction to their social involvement, and an evasion of the real problems. 'We can not find solutions through our social commitment, so we will solve our difficulties through the Holy Spirit', was their perspective. Then at the other end of the spectrum were those whose commitment to conscientization had led them to armed rebellion—notably the group of university students turned guerrillas led by Nestor Paz Zamora, who died from exhaustion and starvation in the Teoponte area in 1970. 'A very high ideal, but very low efficiency', commented Albo. 'Conscientization must go hand in hand with a rational use of techniques.' His own philosophy can be summed up in his allusion to the words of Loyola. 'We have to work in such a way as if everything depends on *us—our* work; and then we have to trust that we have God working

with us in everything. And usually the problem with the
charismatics is that they forget the first part; and the problem
with other people who become atheists is that they forget the
second part. But if we are really part of the plan of God we
have to do all we can ourselves, and realize that this is our
job here, because of God's will; and that we have God working
with us in it.'

This apparent dichotomy between theology of liberation
and the charismatic movement was deplored by Mortimer
Arias, Bishop of the Methodist church in Bolivia. 'Jesus
Christ came in the Spirit, and he came to liberate, so here
together you have the charismatic and the liberating dimensions of the Gospel. In Jesus Christ it is one, but we have put
asunder what God has joined together. Some while ago I
raised the question: 'Why can't we have a cross-fertilization
of the two, since in Jesus Christ we have both?" Instead,
however, we find a polarization of the two. But from the
point of view of my responsibility as a bishop of the church,
I believe we have to keep open both windows.'

Arias is a Urugaian, but like Albo he has a long record
of service in Bolivia. Although their approach to peasant
problems may be different, they share a deep concern for the
life of the Aymara people who live on this windswept plateau.
This concern had taken Arias to a pueblo called Turrini, 100
miles out of La Paz along the northern side of Lake Titicaca.
The only way of getting to see him was by a bus that left
town at 4 a.m.

I had tried to a get a ticket the previous night, but all seats
were sold and their occupants were already in their places
and settling down for the night. So it was a case of pot-luck
next morning, and after a bad start, when the driver ran into
a taxi, leading to a furious altercation, we set off up the wind-
ing road that leads out of the La Paz gorge. I had been in
crowded buses in Latin America, but here it didn't even
matter whether your feet were on the floor—you were imprisoned and held upright by a suffocating jam of humanity.
Just past the police check-point on the altiplano, the driver

stopped again, this time to help a friend whose truck had broken down. Dawn came to reveal the snow-capped Andes on the horizon, and in the foreground a score of motionless figures squatting under their ponchos around the bus. Uncertain when we were likely to move again, and, truth to tell, vastly relieved to escape from the claustrophobically dense atmosphere of the bus, I thumbed a lift in the back of a passing pick-up, sharing the swirling dust and vibration with a group of exhuberant youngsters off for a day's fishing by the shores of the lake. Arriving at Anchoraimes, I made for the Methodist hospital, where Dr Evaristo and his wife made me welcome and gave me coffee before providing me with a jeep for the last few miles to Turrini.

We drove up a wide, open valley of arable land, dotted with mud brick dwellings, a view of the vast upland lake in the distance. At the head of the valley, groups of people were sitting on the parched grass, most of them well muffled in brightly coloured scarves and knitted caps, in spite of the sunshine. One group, composed entirely of men, was perched on the brow of a hillock, listening to one of their number addressing them in Aymara. Seated among them was Mortimer Arias.

Apparently I had arrived at an historic moment in the history of the Bolivian Methodist church. Practically all the people in the Turrini area were Methodists, many of them having joined the church in the past few years. Now for the first time, Arias explained, a basic discussion document, on evangelism, had been translated into an indigenous language, and the Aymara peasants gathered on that hilltop were able to listen and discuss the meaning of their faith in their own dialect rather than in Spanish. This reflected a new concern for the church to be incarnated in the Bolivian reality.[3] The Aymara congregations are the majority in our church,' said Arias, 'but we have always discussed in Spanish. For instance, our "Manifesto to the Nation" five years ago was never translated into Aymara or Quechua. So it becomes a basic document for the leadership of the church, but not for the people at the grass-roots. But today, the people here are taking these theses on evangelism in their own language and trying to understand and interpret what it means for them in their own situation. And we hope we will receive some feedback which will lead to action.'

Arias was cautious about the place of theology of liberation in the Methodist church in Bolivia. 'We have been doing theology in our own way—home-made theology, where maybe some influences or ideas coming from the ecumenical world or Latin American theology have had their impact; but we are not deliberately trying to take theology of liberation and see what it means to us and apply it to our church—this is not the way we work.' It is clear, however, from a reading of the 1970 Manifesto to the Nation, that its interpretation of the gospel and its application to man in society places Bolivian Methodist leadership within the same stream of liberation theology to which Gutierrez has given expression. 'The God whom we know in the Bible, is a liberating God, a God who destroys myths and alienations, a God who inter-venes in history in order to break down the structures of injustice and who raises up prophets in order to point out the way of justice and mercy.'[4] And it was significant that Arias was just beginning to develop a study course for more advanced church leaders on theology of liberation, focusing on the thoughts of Gutierrez, Segundo and Rubem Alves. But the very word 'liberation' had to be used with great care: 'the word is a bad word to people in the intelligence service, and "third world priest" is the worst thing you can say about someone; or membership of ISAL*—that's enough for anybody to be kicked out of the country. So—what can you do res-ponsibly under captivity? What is a Christian supposed to do? Well, I find that in the O.T. most of the best theology was done under captivity. Just think of the time of Manasseh, when all the prophets were killed. There was no public prophetic utterance. But a prophetic party was working on

* Church and Society in Latin America.

Deuteronomy preparing the model for the future. Fifty years later, it became the basis for the new nation, under Josiah. And think of Jeremiah or Isaiah. And maybe this is the one thing that remains to be done, under captivity, or between captivity and liberation.'

The reality of which Arias spoke was forcibly brought home to me next day when I travelled east to Cochabamba, the second city of Bolivia. The Methodist pastor here had recently returned from the U.S.A. after two years in exile, a penalty he had suffered for his work among the campesinos of Eastern Bolivia. The Banzer government had allowed him to return on condition that he sign a document renouncing any involvement in political activity. But a pastor is still a pastor, and he was one of the first at the local hospital in January '74 when numbers of wounded peasants were brought in, casualties of an army attack on the barricades they had erected in protest against the sudden and massive rise in the cost of living. Over 100 peasants had been killed in the action, according to the report[5] published by the church's 'Justice and Peace' committee a few weeks before I arrived in Bolivia. Publication had badly strained relations between church and government, the latter seizing all the copies they could lay their hands on, and forbidding further sales. But one at least was to be had under the counter in La Paz, and in slightly cloak and dagger fashion it was handed over to me, a potentially dangerous item among my papers until I was safely across the Brazilian border. But I wasn't sticking my neck out nearly as much as the youngster who procured it for me. He was openly engaging in the campaign for signatures to pressure the government for a reversal of the order to deport two of the foreign priests on the committee that had published the offending document. It was through his invitation that I found myself spending a weekend at a young people's camp in central Bolivia, where swimming, soccer and volleyball provided the relaxation from group discussion of 'liberation theology for beginners'. The camp leader—let's call him Juan —a highly intelligent and articulate young Bolivian, knew

Nestor Paz, and while sharing his passionate idealism, possessed a much more realistic approach to the political situation
in his country, and a more sober appraisal of the ways in
which change can come about. For example, his girl friend,
an equally determined and intelligent person, had a brother
who held a commission in the Bolivian army—and she was
working steadily on him. But clearly, for him, a time of
captivity was not simply a time for elaborating a theology
for the future, as his carefully thought-out leadership of the
camp programme demonstrated. Not that it was all earnest
discussion: some of the songs sung round the camp-fire with
typical South American enthusiasm would remain in the
youngsters' memory when details of theological discussion
had long been forgotten:

> 'Let's spread it around,
> That the land is ours,
> It's yours and his,
> Pedro's and Maria's, Juan's and José's.
>
> Have you never thought of this?
> That if the hands are ours,
> Then the fruit of our labour is ours too.
>
> If my song troubles anyone who passes by,
> You can bet he's either one of the bosses, or
>   a gringo.'

(This last with broad grins in my direction—but Juan was
quick to add that there are gringos and gringos!)

The songs around the camp-fire that night were interspersed
with folk dances presented by groups of girls from various
regions of the country, and as the graceful movements of the
lithe young figures were lit up by the glow of the fire, the
harsh political realities of Bolivia seemed a world away.

The camp site lay in the Cochabamba valley, fertile and
sylvan, with its backcloth of the Andean foothills, midway
between the altiplano of Western Bolivia, and the eastern

lowlands around Santa Cruz. This latter area is the most rapidly developing in the whole country, and the movement of colonization in Santa Cruz state is similar to that in North-west Paraná, across the Brazilian border. But whereas the Paraná boom has largely been built on coffee, in Santa Cruz the main products are sugar, cotton—and oil. A rich iron deposit has also just begun to be exploited. It's a region of such potential prosperity that, as the taxi-driver from the Santa Cruz airport cheerfully remarked, the government in La Paz is half-afraid that it's going to have another Biafra on its hands. The region attracts peasants in large numbers from the altiplano—both migrant workers, who come to harvest the cotton and sugar in order to supplement their income, but who find the warm and fever-ridden lowlands too uncongenial a habitat for permanent settlement, and colonists who are prepared to attempt entirely new surroundings and settle on a more permanent basis under the direction of the National Institute of Colonization.

Montero, north of Santa Cruz, is the centre of a large tract of land being developed under this government scheme, which enjoys the co-operation of the Iglesias Unidas, a committee of Catholics, Methodists and Mennonites who work together in an extensive programme of practical aid for the colonists. Seven years ago, American missionaries from these three groups found they were on the same wavelength and working for the same objectives—so the United Church Committee was formed, following a spontaneous united response to the needs of flood victims in 1968. Harry Peacock, the Methodist president, believes that in this situation you can do more by pursuing objectives without the use of 'dirty' words like liberation and conscientization—it's better to speak of developing people's natural resources and initiatives. He is fully aware of the ambiguity of co-operation with the authorities, but for him the criterion of whether or not to stay on was brought sharply into focus by a wise old believer who had simply asked: 'Will the people suffer more if you stay, or if you go?' Talking with Harry about his work, it is hard to

believe he and his Mennonite and Catholic colleagues made
the wrong decision. Some achievements are measurable—
areas of land cleared with the help of chain saws, the numbers
of houses and latrines built, the artesian wells drilled. Others
may take more time to evaluate. In one community, before
the provision of a well, people had been obliged to walk a
long distance for stagnant water. The day the well was finished
and the water flowed, the people came together, the band of
drum and flute and guitar played, and after a hymn the community leader voiced the prayer of thanksgiving of the people.
This festival of the water has become an annual event. In
another community, a group of about forty sat round discussing their chance of a new start, and said: 'We have the
opportunity to determine the kind of environment we want
our children to grow up in; and the things we want for our
children we have to produce now.' One of these things is
community worship, which they organize themselves; and if
an experienced visitor is present, whether Catholic priest or
Methodist layman, he is invited to participate. Community
schools are another of the concerns of the Iglesias Unidas.
Harry advocates discussing with the people their own
priorities for curriculum development, and encouraging them
to recruit from their own number the individuals with the
most highly developed skills in a particular field—carpentry,
sheep-shearing, market gardening. His Mennonite colleague
insists on the basic literary skills also as an essential foundation, and this was the particular concern of some young
Mennonite volunteers from the U.S.A.

The work at Montero has attracted the support both of
Oxfam and Christian Aid, the latter channelling funds
through the Commission of Study and Social Action of
the Catholic church to the parish at Montero. This project
is particularly concerned with the thousands of migrant
workers who make the journey annually from the altiplano
to work in the cotton and sugar harvests, and who until
recently have found themselves in the hands of middlemen
who hire them out on contract to the big farmers. This system

resulted in a ruthless exploitation of peasants from the Andes. Now, however, workers are being encouraged to make the annual migration in whole communities, so maintaining their cohesion and, by appointing their own spokesman, putting them in a much better bargaining position for wages and conditions. This project, impressively documented and detailed, is helping to do for migrant peasants who come eastwards what Javier Albo and CIPCA are doing for the people of the altiplano; it is all part of the same process of awareness-building which will eventually enable the Bolivian peasant to live a freer and more genuinely human life. It is theology of liberation in action.

CHAPTER THREE

Brazilian Miracle

> I am trying to send men to heaven, not sheep. And
> certainly not sheep with their stomachs empty and
> their testicles crushed.
>
> *Dom Helder Camara*

THE Caravelle of the Brazilian 'Cruzeiro do Sul' airline was
flying over the forest of the Bolivian lowlands, some way
north of the Nancahuazu gorge where Guevara was captured
and killed in 1967. But long before we crossed the river
Paraguai and headed for Campo Grande in Mato Grosso,
the sense of homecoming engulfed me like a tidal wave. The
day's edition of *O Estado de Sâo Paulo* was in the paper rack,
conversation in the magical clarity of Brazilian Portuguese
was all around me, and the first refreshment offered was a
bottle of Guaraná, the delicious Brazilian soft drink. I remarked to the stewardess that it was the first in five years.
'Five years away from Brazil?' she exclaimed incredulously—
'let me bring you another!'

At Congonhas airport in São Paulo, the Brazilian talent
for making the stranger welcome was equally apparent. I had
been unable to draw cash on a letter of credit in Santa Cruz,
and had spent my last dollar on the air ticket to Brazil. In
São Paulo, the banks had closed for the day. I still had to
make Curitiba, 250 miles south, but I was penniless. At the
Transbrasil desk, I asked for a ticket on credit. 'Very unusual',
commented the desk clerk—'and anyway, the last plane to
Curitiba is fully booked. But I'll see what I can do.' He did,
and thirty minutes later I was on the plane, on the strength
of a promise to pay at the Curitiba agency the following day.

From the airport to the Paraná capital is a drive of twenty
minutes, past the characteristic pines, their trunks tall and
bare like a huge telegraph pole, topped with branches curving
out horizontally like some giant Jewish candlestick. Approach-

ing the city you could see the economic miracle embodied:
new buildings in the brash, adventurous style of Brazilian
architecture; the latest models from vw in São Paulo stream-
ing down the new urban freeways, while other streets had been
converted into pedestrian precincts, where the shops bulged
with all the goods and gadgetry of the consumer society.
Paraná is the leading coffee-producing state in Brazil, and one
of the most progressive areas in the whole country. With its
high proportion of European immigrants and its equable
climate on the plateau above the Sierra do Mar, Curitiba
enjoys the same atmosphere of middle-class prosperity as
Campinas, the city fifty miles from São Paulo where Rubem
Alves lives. After spending some days renewing old friend-
ships in Curitiba, I travelled north again to Campinas, to talk
with the man described as the 'prophet' of theology of
liberation.

His home is a pleasant suburban villa not far from the
Castelo, a landmark of Campinas, and just a block away
from the Presbyterian Seminary where he once studied. It is
one of the ironies of the present theological climate of Brazil
that a man who is probably the ablest theologian in his
country, and who would be glad to lecture free of charge in
his old seminary, is not welcome there.

When I rang, he answered the door—an athletic figure in
yellow T-shirt and rust coloured jeans, with patrician features,
expressive and mobile, framed with curly greying hair and
sideburns. The only other occupant of the room where he
welcomed me was a small cocker spaniel—'I bought him from
an American missionary', he volunteered. Lighting his pipe,
he settled into an armchair. 'What would you like to know?'

He told me first about his spiritual pilgrimage, which typifies the experience of many of his contemporaries. He spent
his childhood in a small town in the Brazilian interior, but
when he was eleven, the family moved to the city. At once
he found himself in a strange and threatening world, and as
a 'country boy' in a city school he found it difficult to make
friends. During his teens, he took refuge in a fundamentalist

expression of Christian faith and, as a result of a 'revival' mission, applied to the Presbyterian Seminary in Campinas, with the ideal of becoming a sort of Brazilian Billy Graham.

But at the seminary, he rediscovered the experience of community lost since those small town days of his early childhood. And the fundamentalist language he had adopted as a refuge against the harsh reality of loneliness suddenly became superfluous and obsolete. Here were a group of people prepared to share their questions and their weaknesses, a fellowship that held one together when the foundation of certainties that had seemed unassailable began to crumble. The other main factor in the shift of perspective was the birth of awareness of the social, political and economic realities of the country. 'A fundamentalist mentality', remarked Alves, 'does not have the capacity to process this data.' But this awakening to the realities of the Brazilian situation coincided with the arrival at the seminary of teachers well qualified to interpret this reality to his students. In 1953, Richard Shaull, who had just been thrown out of Colombia, joined the staff. He provided Rubem and his fellow students with the theological instruments to help them understand the social responsibility of the Christian, to realize that being a Christian and being responsible in society are related. At the same time, Alves experienced a rejection of the traditional type of Brazilian protestantism which seeks to save man out of this world. Bonhoeffer's 'holy worldliness' spoke powerfully to him as he began to understand the Bible as 'an unfaltering celebration of life and its goodness', and the world itself as the object of the church's redemptive task.[1]

It seemed to him, in the enthusiasm of a young man leaving the seminary for his first pastorate, that no one could fail to understand and share this perspective. But during his early ministry, in a Presbyterian church in the interior of the state of Minas Gerais, he discovered that the strength of the institutional church to defend its traditional interpretation of the gospel was greater than he had realized. The older generation of pastors branded men like Alves not only as religious heretics, but as political subversives as well. The community of freedom and love, the church they looked for, could not be identified with the institutional church, which had grown too much like a dinosaur for adaptation and change.

'The fifties were a very traumatic experience for the church, for various reasons', he explained. 'One was the appearance of a new generation, who began to say different things. They were represented not only by men who'd been through the seminary, but by the powerful lay movement of young Presbyterians. They were very critical of the church; and one of the criticisms was that the leaders of the church were in no state to speak about what was happening in the world, because they had no training for it. They were only trained to visit church members, to pray, to preach on Sundays, and they'd never bothered to understand politics or economics or sociology. All this posed a threat to the older generation, who organized themselves to eliminate it, and when the crunch came, the young people's movement was suppressed. This was in 1957. Since then the church has gone through a series of purges, the inquisitors of the previous one becoming in their turn the victims of the next witch-hunt.'

Not surprisingly, many young pastors left the church in sheer frustration. As Alves puts it, 'Our ecclesiastical frustration produced a secular humanism. Instead of theology, sociology. Instead of the church, the world. Instead of God, man.' It was towards the end of this period that Alves went to Princeton to study for his doctor's degree, and when he returned from the U.S.A., he broke with the organized church. 'I'd reached the conclusion that I wanted to earn my living like any other person. I didn't want to be dependent on the church, because I realized that if I did so, I would completely lose my ability to think and write. The ideal of the full-time minister is a total disaster, because the pastor becomes domesticated by the institutional realities of the church, because he is dominated financially.'

This shift of activity from the pastorate to teaching, from theology to sociology (he teaches sociology at the University of Campinas) brought with it a new interest in politics. 'Our gods died; and they were exchanged for heroes. Politics became our religion ... but our heroes died also.' Alves is understandably reticent about this aspect of his pilgrimage, but one is left to infer that the political climate of Brazil from 1964 onwards left no room for manoeuvre here either. In the face of ecclesiastical reaction and political repression, the only option left seemed a withdrawal into the private world of home, family, friends, work and leisure.

In this situation, the one virtue that must be preserved at all costs is hope, as a bulwark against meaninglessness and despair. This is the basic theme of his two main published works, *A Theology of Human Hope*[2] and *Tomorrow's Child*.[3] In a foreword to the former book, Harvey Cox hails Alves as the voice of the Third World of enforced poverty, hunger, powerlessness and growing rage. But the situation from which he writes is very different from that of Gutierrez; in spite of its cost in terms of political repression and the domination of foreign investment, the Brazilian economic miracle has achieved an affluent standard of living for millions (even if still a minority of the Brazilian population), raising the kind of problems for which Marcuse has a greater relevance than Marx. The possibility of human freedom and creativity in a technological- and consumer-oriented society (policed, to be sure, by a ruthless apparatus of terror)[4] is the question Alves poses. 'The problem that each one faces today in Brazil in urban zones', he says—'the concrete problem isn't liberation, but how to make more money! In other words, the pattern of capitalist society of the U.S. and Europe is already our pattern. I see one of the urgent tasks of preaching as precisely the criticism of this pattern of affluence that is establishing itself.' His preoccupation is with Paul Lehmann's question: 'What does it take to make and to keep human life human in the world?'[5] Hope is the question mark that the community of faith places over the inhumanity of our present society; it is a hope that can be characterized as 'messianic humanism', a hope which recognizes the humanizing intervention of God in history, and which sees the present, however unpromising conditions may appear, as pregnant with a better tomorrow. Alves would agree with Emilio Castro's way of putting it: 'Even when our human eyes cannot see the way out of the maze, we are sure there *is* a way out, and that the moment will come when we leave our exile and set out for the promised land.' This understanding of Biblical history is in contrast to the political humanism he defines as: 'humanistic messianism', the action of man within history to achieve his liberation by his own power. This hope is not for a *Deus ex machina*, a liberation that breaks in from beyond, but a liberation achieved through man's action in protest against the slavery of the present. *A Theology of Human Hope* explores the relationship between these two concepts.

Since writing his first book, however, a shift has occurred in Alves' thought. 'Theology of liberation was written when we thought that we were in an Exodus situation', he said. 'I don't believe we are in such a situation. We're in a situation of captivity.' And in *Tomorrow's Child*, he confesses his pessimism about ever seeing the promised land. But 'we must live by the love of what we will never see'.[6] And this means continuing to nourish the seeds of hope in community.

I asked him where he saw signs of these genuine communities of hope in Brazil. 'You've probably heard of what's happening in the Catholic church', he replied, 'the grass-roots communities. These represent an attempt to break with the traditional model of the church which administers the sacraments for a future life, in favour of a church in which communities address themselves to the very concrete problems of their situation. They are discovering tactics of action which only *can* be discovered by the local group. There's a curious paradox in life in Brazil today. On the one hand, because of the pressures of modern life, and conditions of work, the experience of community encounter is becoming increasingly difficult. People are not available for community encounter because they are so tired from their function in the system that when they have spare time they want to remain on their own.

On the other hand, a tremendous nostalgia for community is being created. So you get a series of experiments—e.g. the "cursillo" type of revival in the Catholic church—it's scientifically programmed but theologically and politically very conservative—yet it expresses a nostalgia for togetherness and the need for a meaningful community as a point of reference.'

What of the role of the Protestant churches within this pattern? In Alves' view, the Protestant presence in Latin America had a particular relevance at a time when the Catholic church was characterized by paganism, superstition, and support for the *status quo*. But even in this period, conversion to Protestantism involved a heavy price in terms of cultural uprooting. 'The Brazilian who became a Protestant ceased to be a Brazilian. The aesthetic pattern changed—instead of the Samba, he sang those hymns of Sankey to organ accompaniment.' Alves regards this process of alienation from Brazilian culture as a serious matter.

But even if formerly this was a price worth paying, can it be justified today? Why did Protestantism come to Brazil? To be sure, there were economic reasons—imperialism, expansion, and the missionary expansion went hand in hand with imperialist and colonial expansion. But from the point of view of the church, the missionaries came to convert the Catholic pagans. To win Brazil for Christ meant to de-Catholicize Brazil, to Protestantize Brazil.

Today, the same situation just does not exist. 'The Catholic church today is much more Protestant than the Protestant churches. There's much more liberty, a more critical spirit—more akin to the Protestant spirit of Paul Tillich. Seeing what the Holy Spirit is doing with the Catholic church, I ask myself, have I the right to quarrel with the Holy Spirit?—to insist on my Protestantism? So for some people, Protestantism has no further mission to fulfil; or if it has, it is one not of polemics, but of service, in a supporting role to the Catholic church; not looking for the growth of the Protestant churches, but to help the Catholic church to become more Christian,[7] more open. This may appear a great scandal to some Protestants! But so far as I'm concerned, when I speak of the possibilities of renewal and of sowing seeds of hope, I'm not interested in sowing in the Protestant churches. I'm not saying it's not important, but it's not for me personally. This ground is too full of stones. In fact I haven't made the choice, it's been made for me.' He spelt out what he meant. 'There's a congregation near here, and the members are mostly people I knew when I was a theological student. Occasionally I go to church. I find it gives them great pleasure when I go: "Rubem Alves is coming back to the church." But there's something else. They want my presence—but they don't want me to say anything. My talk is disturbing. What they would like is the silent presence of Rubem Alves. So the church has already made the choice for me. I can't choose not to speak.'

Helder Camara, like Rubem Alves, is Brazilian. They speak the same language, live in the same country, share a common concern that theology should be tested in the crucible of the Brazilian reality. But the distance that separates them is not merely the geographical one. The 1,500 miles from São Paulo to Recife involves the transition also from the industrialized and developed south to the under-developed and drought-ridden north-east. If the problems Alves wrestles with are those of affluence, the world of Helder Camara is the correlative of this—the massive poverty at the broad base of the social pyramid which supports the affluent cone.

To visit him, I returned from Campinas to São Paulo, where a bus was leaving for Recife at 8 p.m. It was already dark as we pulled out, and before long I had fallen asleep. When I awoke we were somewhere in the highlands of Minas Gerais; the air was fresh as we stopped for coffee. For most of the journey, the bus hurtled along through the wild scenery on a well-paved road, past occasional outcrops of rock like the Sugar Loaf piled up against the sky. Animated conversation in Portuguese, or an occasional snatch of a Brazilian love-song from a euphoric Baiano returning home, provided some diversion. The following morning we're driving through

63

Bahia. We stop at the bridge of the vast São Francisco river, the gateway to Sergipe, where a boy has a wayside stall of green coconuts for 2 cruzeiros apiece. He slashes off the top with his machete, and the cool liquid is like nectar to a dry throat. Once in Sergipe, the land takes on the parched look of the Brazilian north-east, although the bad lands of the worst drought areas are further into the *Sertão*. Soon the landscape is relieved by the green of the massive sugar cane plantations. We pass a lorry loaded with cane—thin, spindly sticks of it compared with the sturdy type produced further south. Forty-four hours after leaving São Paulo, we enter the capital of Pernambuco, centre of the diocese of Olinda and Recife, of which Dom Helder is the archbishop.

I arrived not knowing if he was in town, but within two hours, through the good offices of a friendly Irish parish priest, we were being introduced. A short man, balding, with a lined face and heavy pouches under expressive eyes, he gives an impression of simplicity, but great authority and power. 'You're a Baptist?' he said after the customary Brazilian hug of welcome—'I'm at home with Baptists! In the U.S.A. they gave me the Martin Luther King prize for my efforts for non-violent change.' Yes, of course we could arrange a time for an interview. His programme for tomorrow wasn't worked out yet, but a phone call after mass at 7 a.m. would fix it.

We met the next afternoon in his archbishop's 'palace'—the couple of rooms at the back of the Igreja das Fronteiras, the down-town church where he celebrates mass daily at 6 a.m. whenever he is in residence. His study, where he receives a constant stream of callers, was barely furnished—a picture of a Brazilian peasant on one wall; a straw crucifix on another; bookshelves lined with theology, sociology and politics, including several large volumes on Gandhi. On his desk, a photo of Pope John, the first pope to speak affectionately of his 'separated brethren'.

I asked him how he reacted to Alves' view of the Protestant role in Brazil. 'Well,' he replied, 'I'd say that sometimes the presence of Protestant missionaries can be a tremendous asset.

I like working with American missionaries' (he broke into his puckish smile) 'because I'm often called a communist, but if I'm also co-operating with Americans—well, it's not so easy to call an American a communist!'[8] He considers that while there's just a small group of Catholics preaching the Gospel in an 'incarnated' way, people can say the Catholic church has diverged from the Gospel; so he appreciates the support of Anglicans, Lutherans, Presbyterians, Baptists, Methodists —'if all of us, brothers in Christ, give this witness, the more difficult it will be to say that this is a distortion of the Gospel'.

The need for an incarnated gospel is nowhere more apparent than in the Brazilian north-east. While in Recife, I talked with Marta, a woman deserted by her husband and living with her five children in a shack in one of the many shanty towns. Or rather, four children, because when I saw her she had just buried her youngest child, a victim of dysentery.

'How long was he ill?' I asked.

'About fifteen days.'

'Did you give him medicine?'

'Oh yes, we never lacked for medicine, the lady I work for gave me plenty.'

'And when that didn't work, what about a doctor?'

'How could I take him to a doctor? That would have cost me £7. I earn £12 a month to feed and clothe my family. So I thought, if the child is mine, I'll keep him; if not, God will take him.'

Marta's story typifies not just the endemic poverty and lack of medical care—Brazilian government figures calculate that 15 per cent of the population, i.e. 15 million people, are without any medical care whatsoever; it typifies also the passive, accepting resignation that has its roots in the traditional understanding, or misunderstanding, of Christian faith.

While recognizing the blame attaching to the church for the soporific effect of its preaching in the past, Helder Camara attacks this slave mentality of the people as strenuously as he denounces the unjust policies of the government, and the economic domination which the rich world exerts over the underdeveloped nations.

'We men of the church', he said, 'have been so preoccupied in maintaining authority and the social order that we didn't suspect that the social order masks a terrible disorder, a stratified disorder. For centuries, we were concerned with a very passive presentation of Christianity. We preached patience, obedience, respect for authority; we spoke of suffering, we reminded people of the suffering of Christ, and we finished up by saying (this was the opium of the people!) that the sufferings here on earth are so ephemeral, and eternal happiness so great, that all this would be forgotten in a flash.

'But gradually it became clear that we couldn't go on preaching Christianity like this. Social injustice was becoming ever more blatant; so much so, that at Medellin in Colombia in 1968, at the conference of Latin American bishops,[9] we denounced the presence in Latin America of an internal colonialism. It's not just foreign colonialists who come to exploit our people, but the privileged of the continent who maintain their wealth at the expense of the penury—it's not just poverty, but sheer penury—of millions of their fellow citizens.

'Today, after these centuries of a very passive presentation of Christianity, when we arrive in any working-class area, we encounter the results of our preaching...a situation of near fatalism, or indeed absolute fatalism. So after winning people's confidence, I start like this:

' "But how can you live here? How can you bring up your children in all this squalor and filth?"

' "But that's life, Bishop! You've got to accept the will of God!"

' "But God doesn't want squalor. Squalor is an insult to our Creator and Father! And anyway, it's men who create injustice, and we're the ones who've got to do something about it."

' "But what can we do? What on earth can we do?"

' "Obviously, by yourselves you can't do anything. But

what about your neighbours, your community? You've got to make a start. You've got to meet together to face your problems, here in the community."

' "But that's the government's job!" '

' "If you wait for the government to do everything you'll remain in your poverty for ever. Now, get together for good, get together constructively, get together to begin to face your problems, and then you can go to the government to say what you've done—not as beggars, but as citizens to insist on your rights, and demand that the government should come and help you complete what you've started, which you can't finish by yourselves." '

'We call the work conscientization. We try to awaken a critical awareness, to get people to analyse the facts, to look not simply at what is happening, but at the roots of what is happening. Above all, to look for solutions. But this work is regarded with disfavour by governments and the privileged. It is misinterpreted. They call it subversion, agitation, communism.' He still receives threatening phone calls, and his phone is still tapped. The government do their best to muzzle him—he has no access to the media—and to harass his assistants. There have been arbitrary arrests and disappearances. Was it dangerous work? I asked Abdelazes de Moura, Camara's research assistant. 'Dangerous and then some', was the reply.[10]

Dom Helder had introduced me to Moura at the end of our interview, and we arranged to meet on the following day. As this was Sunday, I would have the opportunity of spending an afternoon with a local group in a working-class suburb, and to see in practice the work of awareness building at grass-roots level that Camara insists on.

Moura is a dynamic young man in his early thirties, with an analytical mind, a friendly disposition, and a quick sense of humour. Sharing the ecumenical outlook of his chief, he has acquired an empathic understanding of the Pentecostals[11] that few Catholics, and perhaps few main-line Protestants, have been able to achieve. Not only has he a warm appreciation of their positive contribution—their directness, the ability of their preachers to speak the language of the people, their evangelistic fervour, their freedom in worship, the sense of community and belonging they convey to the individual member—he has deliberately fostered these qualities among the Catholic grass-roots communities that he and his colleagues have developed.

He is not, however, uncritical of the negative aspects of their witness—their Biblical literalism, their individualistic concept of salvation, and their other-worldly pietism that adopts the attitude 'I'm in the world but I'm not of the world.'[12] This leads to a sublimation of their protest against the harsh conditions of life. Yet these Pentecostals, the vast majority from the poorest social class, are the very people who feel in their flesh the thick end of the stick of the 'social disorder'. If only their protest could be rescued from its projection on to the life to come, and harnessed to tackle the real problems of this life! 'The typical Pentecostal is the poor peasant or worker who sees his child die of hunger and resigns himself with the thought "It's another little angel in heaven". Instead of this, couldn't the poor man ponder that his child died because he couldn't buy milk or medicine?—and from there, go on to ask *why* he can't buy these things? whether it's just that he can't buy them, and who are the people responsible for this unjust situation? And finally, ask himself what he can do to improve the situation and commit himself to improve it?'

Moura goes on to ask how the Catholic church, and the other more theologically articulate churches, can help the Pentecostals to evolve and move in the direction of greater social involvement—a more genuinely 'incarnated' gospel. How establish dialogue? He believes that it's no use trying to bludgeon them with theological argument. Dialogue on this level is impossible, because traditional theology cannot speak the language of the people, and if the Pentecostals attempt to play our theological word game, they'll only become contaminated with our intellectualizing vices. 'It's better, at least as a first step, that the Pentecostals stay where they are and see whether the other churches can't take root among the people.' The only effective dialogue, the only effective argument, will be by example.

The Pentecostal will not be convinced by fair words. No one will persuade him to get mixed up in politics—unless he sees a genuine Christian of the same social class involved in the trade union struggle. No one will convince him that the return of Christ is related to building *this* world—unless he sees a fervent missionary community engaged in shaping history. No one will convince him he ought to abandon his fundamentalism—unless he meets preachers who can speak the language of the people, giving a deeper meaning to revelation.

'This is the sort of thing I mean', Moura told me. 'There's a small rural community not far from here, with a very lively Assemblies of God congregation. It was here that a group of Catholics began a programme of evangelism. First, they decided to rebuild a small chapel that was falling down. That was their first job; and when it was habitable, they began their meetings, with fairly traditional services. But gradually they became aware of other needs in the community. One of these was the problem of literacy. So first they made a survey of the 500 homes in the area, and they found no less than 200 illiterates—adults who couldn't even sign their name. So they began literacy classes in four separate schools.

'As this work was developing, a law was passed guaranteeing a pension for rural workers of sixty-five and over. The law itself was simple enough, but the problem of documentation for the individuals concerned was extremely complicated —in rural areas people just don't possess documents! So they repeated the census of all the homes, this time to discover which of the old people had a right to the pension.

'The next phase in community development was a request to the municipal authorities to rebuild a bridge and make up a road that had become impassable during the winter. Naturally among those who benefited from all this were some Pentecostals. In fact, the Catholics had already drawn some of the Pentecostals into the group which discussed the planning of these various stages of the programme. And they began to ask: "Why don't we go in for this kind of thing in our church? Why don't we look after the welfare of our neighbour?" All this is by no means unique—it's happened in various places. Elsewhere, an elderly member of the Baptist church, Sr Magalhães, began to be aware of the social relevance of the gospel. A man with a wide experience of life who had suffered a lot, worked on a sugar plantation and known poverty, he saw the way some Catholics were involving themselves with the question of wage claims—the sugar refinery wasn't even paying the minimum salary prescribed by law. So as a Baptist, he decided that this was a question that ought to be discussed in his own church too; the gospel demanded this of him.'

This discovery of the social relevance of the gospel had been made by the small group of Catholic laymen and women who met with Moura at the back of a church in Prazeres that afternoon. Topics to be included in the local newsheet on social action were the conditions of work of domestic employees; the minimum salary earned by workers; and the state of a local street which the council had begun to repave and then abandoned. This last had created a serious problem. The loose earth thrown on the road had become ground to powder by passing traffic, which threw up a thick cloud of dust over the gardens and houses along the street, constituting a health hazard for the local people. Representations had had no effect; so one night the local action committee got a group of men together who dug deep trenches across opposite ends of the street, effectively diverting the traffic away from the offending dust. Officials from the council had visited the scene, demanding to know who was responsible for this unauthorized obstruction of traffic. 'The people did it' was the only reply they got.

The sense of solidarity and common purpose among the group was impressive. At the end of the discussion period, we stood, linked hands for a moment, and I was invited to lead in prayer. Here was a group of people committed to Christ, to each other, and to the needs of their neighbours. There are many such groups in Recife, linked as spokes to the diocesan hub by means of a radio programme called 'Encounter between brothers', which presented dramatized stories from the Bible and related them to the work initiated by the social action groups. And one of the most hopeful things Moura saw happening was that, at this level of concrete action, Catholics and Protestants were beginning to recognize each other as brothers. As he put it, 'Christian unity isn't going to be decided and directed by the official church, by the statements of committees in Geneva or Rome; it's life itself that will speak!'

This, then, is the considered judgement of a Catholic who has thought deeply on the ecumenical question. Is it a judgement that finds a response among Pentecostals? This depends on the type of Pentecostal. Some massive Pentecostal sects (in common with most Baptists) in Brazil will have nothing to do with ecumenism. The 'Congregação Cristã do Brasil' rejects co-operation with other Pentecostals, let alone with Catholics. There is, however, a strong Pentecostal movement 'Igreja Pentecostal Brasil para Cristo' led by Manoel de Mello, that takes a much more positive line. Mello's church is a member of the World Council of Churches, not because he supports everything the Council stands for, but because he believes that a Christian attitude is one of open dialogue with one's brothers in the faith, and because through the social service arm of the Council his church can more effectively act out his slogan 'Gospel with Bread'. Here at least is one Pentecostal leader who sees clearly the social implications of the Christian message. Hence the Brazil for Christ Movement, together with the National Conference of Brazilian Bishops (Catholics), the Episcopal church, the Methodists and the Presbyterians, are constituent members of CESE, the Ecumenical Agency for Social Service, which has its headquarters in Salvador, the old colonial capital of Brazil and chief city of Bahia.

Enilson Souza, the Presbyterian who runs CESE from an office in down-town Salvador, explained the philosophy behind their work, which is supported by ecumenical agencies such as Christian Aid. The first point was a geographical one: the very fact that the headquarters was located in the north-east of the country symbolized the priorities of CESE. The south had enough resources of its own; it was here, in the north-east, where the need was greatest, that the resources of providing bodies must be concentrated. But secondly, these resources were acceptable only if the deployment of them was firmly in the hands of nationals. Souza made it quite clear that from now on, Brazilians themselves must decide where the priorities lay, and how money was to be allocated—otherwise, they were simply not interested, no matter how genuine the good intentions of would-be donors. For instance, rivers of money had been poured into the Gurupi farming settlement in Maranão State by ecumenical agencies, but because so much of the planning had been done 'from above', and often by foreigners, the local people had failed to assume responsibility, and results had been disappointing in relation to the vast sums invested. By contrast, a similar but more modest project at Damasio had flourished on a much smaller budget, because it involved decision-making at grass-roots level, and had achieved a far greater degree of integration with the surrounding community.[13] Yet when a golden opportunity had arisen to acquire a further piece of land to extend the project, for lack of a relatively small sum of money, the opportunity was lost, since the matter had to be referred to London before funds could be made available. This was the kind of situation that Souza was determined to avoid in future.

He went on to describe one of CESE's priority projects. At Feira de Santana, not far from Salvador and at a strategic point on the road from north to south, CESE had set up a training centre for rural labourers heading south in search of work in industry. The centre provided a medical check-up for the men and their families. It helps them acquire identity documents from government departments (too often in the interior such documents are non-existent, but without them a man cannot be taken on in a factory). It offers a three-month basic training course in one of several trades. Finally it provides a programme of 'awareness-building' which helps to equip a man for the struggle for existence in Brazilian industrial society. For struggle it is. During the decade of the economic miracle, the poorest 40 per cent of the population have had their share of the national wealth reduced from 10 to 8 per cent. The earning power of the minimum salary (the subsistence wage of a large number of the working population) has actually fallen; and while the richest 10 per cent of the population have made sensational gains, infant mortality rates are worsening—even in São Paulo, the very centre of the economic boom.

A worker in Brasilia recently put it like this:

'I am a 37-year-old Brazilian. My wife has had ten children and five are still alive. We used to live in Brasilia, our nation's new capital, because we heard there was work there, and there wasn't any in the small town where we were before. I am in construction work, carrying cement, bricks, water, mixing concrete, moving wooden moulds, and so on.

'I said we used to live in Brasilia. One morning an army truck came to our house. They said we would be moved to a new town that afternoon. Some of our neighbours had already been moved. The soldiers came back, tore down our house, loaded it and us on the truck and drove for over an hour. On this barren hill-top called Ceilandia, they dumped us on a small lot and said it would be ours eventually when we paid for it. They told us to rebuild our house on the back of the lot because we were supposed to build a new brick house on the front. But with no money for food how can we buy bricks?

'Now it takes me two hours to get to work. I have to leave at four in the morning and don't get home until after eight at night. Paying for buses means we cannot buy meat.

'Our side of the town has no running water, although the government has promised it in two or three years. Twice a week the water truck comes and we run after it rolling one of our barrels. By the time it stops there are a lot of barrels waiting for water. Then we take the water home in old olive oil cans and empty them into our other barrel at the side of the house. Finally we roll the barrel home. Sometimes I can't go to work because I must help with the water.

'Last year they told us our children could go to school, but when we took them we did not have the right papers. They told us to come back when we had them, but there is no money to pay for them. I really want my boys to go to school.

'Today the man at the job told me I am not needed any more. I have been working on this building for almost a year. I know he needs workers. A friend of mine says they fire workers before they work a year. If they don't the company must pay more, or there are some benefits. When I work full time I make $57 a month. That doesn't happen very often.

'Last month my cousin moved in with us. There are seven in his family and his daughter has meningitis. They went to the clinic we have, and after seven hours waiting they saw the doctor. He gave them some medicine and said she had to have it to live. Last week they missed their appointment for more medicine and can't get to the doctor for three or four more days.'[14]

Small wonder that the Brazilian Catholic bishops and leaders of the north east have declared:

'The Brazilian miracle has never gained the people's faith, devotion and hope. It has resulted in privileges for the wealthy and suffering for those already being sacrificed.'[15] This was in 1973. More recently, a writer in a little-known periodical asked the question—'Can the "system" undergo such a radical transformation as to distribute more fairly both national income and political power? To achieve this really *would* be a Brazilian miracle!'[16]

CHAPTER FOUR

Southern Cone Military

> The Christian can talk to the Marxist about suffering
> and death in the situation where together they face it.
> *J. Miguez Bonino*

T H E man next to me on the bus south to the Brazilian city
of Porto Alegre was incredulous when I told him I was
bound for Montevideo. 'You're not going into that hornet's
nest?' he asked; 'look at this.' He passed me his newspaper
which carried a report of the projected protest march by
Uruguaian trade unionists on May Day, in spite of a government order forbidding any demonstrations.

If any fleeting concern crossed my mind about getting
caught in the cross-fire of street battles, I need not have
worried. When I arrived in Montevideo early on the morning
of May 1, it was like a city of the dead. Shops, offices, restaur-
ants and bars were closed and shuttered. Scarcely a pedestrian
was to be seen—apart from the occasional men in uniform,
in pairs, apparently out for a stroll. Less unostentatious were
the armoured cars at street corners, and the helicopter
patrolling overhead. Evidently the authorities were taking no
chances. At least on May Day the grip of the military dictatorship on Uruguay was even more evident here than in Bolivia
or Brazil.

'Like everyone else, the Christian has to keep quiet.' Juan
Luiz Segundo, the Uruguaian Jesuit, was talking about his
conviction that socialism is the best political expression of
Christian faith. Yet even if overt political activity was impossible under the present regime, at least the Christian had a duty
to be aware, and to help other people to be aware—within the
family, in one's circle of friends, and in small discussion
groups. It was out of such a discussion group at the Peter

75

Faber Centre in Montevideo that his five-volume work *A Theology for Artisans of a New Humanity* emerged.[1] Similar Jesuit centres had been created in many Latin American countries, originally with the intention of spreading the social doctrine of the church as a bulwark against communism. In some countries, where the church was politically powerful, these centres had become think-tanks for Christian Democrat politicians, and, like the one in Santiago, had been consulted by such men as Frei, a former President of Chile. But in Uruguay, perhaps the most secularized of Latin American countries, the church had little power or privilege; so instead of discussing the theoretical social doctrine of the church, which would have little political impact, the Peter Faber Centre in Montevideo, comprising a small group of students and young professional people, developed what Segundo calls a 'dialogue between theology and reality', an attempt to formulate Christian faith in the light of existing reality. His five-volume work is the result.

It is impossible adequately to summarize the very wide-ranging discussions set out in these volumes. Segundo uses a broader canvas than any other Latin American theologian, bringing to bear on traditional themes of theology valuable insights from psychology, sociology and modern literature. Volume III, 'Our Idea of God', does the same kind of demolition job on Latin American mental idols as *Honest to God* did for many people in Britain. 'Do we ever realize that we may be injecting into our God the base, egotistical values that rule our lives and that are not God at all? Is it not possible that when we say "I believe", we are making an act of faith in capitalism, injustice, suffering and egotism?'[2] But more constructively, 'God is a continuing summons in our lives to a never-ending search for authentic solutions . . . God is the unrest in us that does not allow us to be tranquil and content that keeps prodding us toward the better course that remains ahead of us.'[3] Since God has created man for love in community, in the history we share with God, no love is lost in this world; and it is this phrase 'no love is lost' that runs like a refrain through Segundo's work. No absolute distinction can be made between the church and the world, since all men travel the same road, and it leads them to salvation: it is the road of self-giving through love. But the church is the community of those who *believe* that no love is lost, who know that their trust is well placed, that there is Someone who responds to our faith. In the midst of the human race, there must be people who know the mystery of love, who will meet and dialogue with those who are moving towards the gospel and confronting the questions raised by love. The church is meant to be a sign to the whole of humanity that this self-giving love is the very meaning and purpose of creation. But the church's sign-bearing function can only be fulfilled if it is composed of people committed to this way—and this means a minority church, functioning in society as salt or leaven. Segundo's view of the church has been called elitist, and in a sense it is; but if anyone looks to the church for aristocratic privilege, 'the only aristocracy he will get, if he really wants it, is an aristocracy of self-giving and love that may even entail death.'[4]

Does this insistence on a minority church mean that Segundo sees nothing in popular Latin American religiosity that can be turned to good account?

'Well,' he said, 'It's not only a fact of experience but also of theological principle—in fact, in the thesis I wrote for my doctorate, I tried to establish that it's not a question of characterizing popular religion—whether it's good or bad, hopeful or hopeless. Popular religion, in its beginning, is a compromise between Christianity and the actual political reality; and in Latin America today, the demands of the gospel are being watered down by compromise. The gospel is made cheap by getting mixed up with nationalism, or being offered together with handouts; and that's not Christianity, it's just a way of making things easy, and that's no good either for the salvation or the human promotion of people. For me, mass Christianity is a contradiction in terms; for real Christianity is a demanding Christianity, the Christianity of the cross, which inevitably becomes selective by the very fact of being the most heroic concept in the world. Of course Christianity has to be preached to everyone—this is very important, it's not a question of *our* selection—but it's only a minority which has the personal security to carry out the heroic mission of the church. The universality of the gospel—and here I agree with Moltmann—is not a universality of numbers, but of function—of leaven, or of salt. Those who accept the gospel without it being made easy, and without any coercion, will always be a minority, but an effective minority. The mixture of minorities with majorities has the result that Christianity becomes neither yeast nor anything else within society. Everyone is "Christian", and Christianity means nothing.'

Segundo believes that these effective minorities exist wherever a group of committed Christians who know and trust each other come together to reflect on their real life situation in the light of their common faith. These groups can generate the vision for social change, although the practical means of achieving this is a matter for scientific analysis. Preaching the gospel and promoting better social structures must go hand in hand, since many of the deprived and oppressed people of Latin America, treated as objects by the system, lack even the basic human authenticity of life without which a man cannot genuinely hear the Word of God. This is why so many Christians are for socialism, since they consider that in Latin America at present it offers the best chance of improving structures and raising the level of human life. Hence also the collaboration of Christians and Marxists—depending on the openness or orthodoxy of the Marxist. 'There are some heterodox Marxists who admit that Marx didn't say all there is to say about religion, but that there are other ways of conceiving it.' These, however, were not sentiments to voice openly in President Bordaberry's Uruguay, whose fanatical anticommunism had led to the creation of a totalitarian state. Whether his downfall in the palace revolution of June 12, 1976, will lead to a relaxation of repression and freedom for any of Uruguay's 6,000 political prisoners remains to be seen. Segundo himself has been in prison for his views.

Across the river Plate estuary, in Buenos Aires, a more fundamental change of government has taken place since last year, for at least Isabel Peron's government claimed some measure of popular support. The posters plastered all over the Argentinian capital, depicting 'Isabelita', Peron's third wife, with Peron and Eva looking down on her from the clouds, reflected something of the Peronist aura which still clung to her. But she was, in fact, little more than a puppet, and with the economic situation going from bad to worse, on March 24, 1976, the expected military *coup* took place, bringing to power General Jorge Videla as head of state. The circle of military governments of the southern cone is now complete; and an ominous development since then is that several Catholic priests have become the victims of the right-wing terror squads that operate with apparent impunity.

It was under the shadow of this predictable *coup* that Dr José Miguez Bonino gave me his version of the change that was coming over liberation theology. 'It's like an athlete going in for a 100 metres sprint, and half way through someone shouts to him—the race is 400 metres! and he has to adjust his pace and breathing to a longer haul.' As Vice-Rector of ISEDET (Instituto Superior Evangelico de Estudios Teologicos) in Buenos Aires, he had been involved in the development of theology of liberation from the beginning, and his book *Revolutionary Theology Comes of Age* is perhaps the most comprehensive account of it so far to appear in English. Like Segundo, Miguez is an intellectual; but he is also a Methodist preacher, and his work contains some down-to-earth illustrations reminiscent of a Methodist pulpit. Over lunch, he enlarged on his view of the change of emphasis in liberation theology.

'Think of the way in which liberation theology began', he said, 'An effort of some theologians to reflect on what was happening with people who were engaged in the struggle for liberation in very different places: Brazil, Bolivia, Chile, and so on. Now the struggle for liberation has taken a different form because of the presence of these strong repressive regimes in practically all of Latin America, and a greater awareness of the great power of the present structure, with its ability to implement an ideological repression as well as a political one. Some of the people involved in the struggle are still able to live in this continent, but others have had to leave it; hence Alves' dictum that we are in a state of captivity rather than of Exodus. I agree with him, that the road towards an Exodus looks now a much longer and more painful road.

'This has a number of consequences. For one thing, you see things in a different perspective. If the possibility of a change in the economic and political structure is almost immediately ahead, there's a total concentration on the political aspects, because there's no time for anything else; but when you look to a longer haul, other considerations enter the picture. It's more important now to build up the courage and patience and perseverence that is necessary for a longer struggle; and personal qualities like maturity and inner spiritual resources, together with the building up of communities, become much more important. So I would say that more attention is being given to building up the spiritual life of the church, to devotion and worship, which were to a certain extent "bracketed out" at an earlier phase.

'Again, there was a certain optimism present in some forms of theology of liberation (some, not all, because others were more sober about the changes contemplated), a sense that the strength of the liberation movement would do away with any obstacle. This now is chastened and there's a greater realism. There's also an awareness of the limits of the social and political tools that have to be used but which cannot exhaust the reality that is analysed. The strength of the forces of reaction is much greater than a purely rational analysis of the situation would suggest—for instance, oppressed peoples and classes are much more resigned to their own situation, much less eager for change than one would have expected from a purely class analysis. So you're not struggling merely against flesh and blood, but against a certain power of darkness which escapes a purely sociological or even ideological analysis.

'On the other hand, there are elements of hope that also go beyond a purely rational analysis; this rediscovery of the importance of culture, of religious and spiritual values, to some extent transcends the classical forms of analysis and acquires a larger perspective. These things are becoming more important.'

I found this emphasis on a return to the spiritual dimension of the struggle interesting, since I had heard ISEDET criticized as an intellectual ivory tower somewhat divorced from the churches at the grass-roots, and asked Miguez how he reacted to this criticism.

'There is no reason to deny that ISEDET and the theology of liberation may seem remote from some local congregations', he replied. 'But the question has to be asked "where are the grass-roots?" Is it the Methodist congregations in Argentina, basically small middle-class groups, usually quite remote from the people in their own neighbourhood—no one knows them in this neighbourhood, they form an exclusive religious club —is that the grass-roots? When a minister of a church is related to a trade union, is he more, or less, related to the grass-roots? It is a problem of definition, and this is so particularly with the Roman Catholic exponents of theology of liberation. Many of them have problems with their church, with the hierarchy of their church, or sometimes with the seminary. But most of them are working in the slums. Are they close to or remote from the grass-roots?

'Still, there's no denying that one of the facts of the new situation is the recognition that there has been a neglect of the churches as such, and that perhaps because the churches on the whole are rather hard and conservative, in the shorter perspective there is a tendency to write them off—but when the revolution comes, then the churches would be forced to face the situation, and *then* would be the time to go back and try to help them face the change. But now in this new situation, a number of people are saying: "We were wrong about this; and although we cannot be confined to the church, it is important to participate in the life of the church and to try to bring the church together within the movement for liberation."[5]

'Another factor is a very interesting reawakening of groups of young people in the church within the past couple of years. In the Methodist church in Argentina, the Young Methodists, almost non-existent three years ago, are now a powerful group organizing themselves quite spontaneously for a programme of study and work. This is not just a local phenomenon—in Chile and Bolivia also, there are groups of young people trying to start afresh.'

On the question of the involvement of a local church in direct political action, Miguez has changed his point of view. 'If you include social action within the definition of "political", there are some things the churches ought to do and can do; for instance, in the defence of human rights, or in the help of people who are marginalized or persecuted in one way or another. But I don't think the church should take too much direct initiative. The great problem of the church is not that it doesn't do enough, but that it doesn't create the kind of concern out of which people will do things. When people become church members, they are vaccinated against concern, or their concern takes very set religious forms, and that tends to satisfy them. The minister's vocation should be to create the kind of climate of love and concern that will generate the participation of the people at different levels and in different forms—the possibilities are endless. But you cannot prescribe the same expression of your political and social concern for a congregation here in this suburb of Buenos Aires, and a congregation up on the altiplano.'

An unexpectedly vivid example of a local congregation in action was to be found at Mendoza, the provincial town some 700 miles west of Buenos Aires and nestling in the shadow of the Andean peaks. The road from the Chilean capital snakes over the Andean pass where the famous Christ of the Andes statue gazes over the Chile/Argentine frontier, and Mendoza is the first Argentine town you come to as you travel east. In September 1973, the small Methodist church there found itself in the path of a trickle of political refugees from Chile, that rapidly turned to a flood. The pastor, Federico Pagura, told me how the church stood up to the impact.

'When the Chilean refugees started to arrive in Mendoza, the World Council of Churches sent us a letter—as they did to many other churches in Argentina—inviting us to undertake a programme of aid for all these people leaving Chile. And the leaders of the Methodist church resolved to accept this challenge. In the beginning, the number of individuals and families arriving was small, but gradually the number grew. At first, we received them in our own homes, but later this became impossible—the sheer weight of numbers created another problem, and we had to find a different solution. This was when the UN intervened and offered us help; and since March '74 we've been working in collaboration with the UN and WCC. Locally, we invited the Lutheran and Catholic churches to co-operate, and this has created a very deep fellowship and a true ecumenism.

'Further, this work has enabled us to create a genuine witness to the gospel. Many of these folk who arrived from Chile had had contact with the churches there during their childhood or adolescence, but the majority had left the churches, in some cases for reasons that one can fully understand. Others still belonged to the churches, especially the Methodist Pentecostal church, together with some Methodists, Lutherans and Baptists. So it has given a better opportunity than for many years past for dialogue about Christian faith. And for our own congregation, it has meant a great shake-up, for many reasons.

'The whole of this building (the church and its adjacent premises) had been very quiet—it was simply used for the service of our small local congregation. Now it's placed at the service of all these refugees. During the week, the place is alive with people, who bring their problems of accommodation, food, health, legal problems, and so on. These problems are tackled individually by the ecumenical social action committee—it's composed of social workers, a lawyer, and a psychologist (who works with children and adults, helping them with problems that result from torture and imprisonment in Chile).

'So we have a job that is growing, and one which the Methodist church has accepted at first with a certain fear. Some have seen it as dangerous work. Some of the more timid members, or those with a more ingrown understanding of their faith, are afraid that it will lead to the police asking questions, or that someone will put a bomb in the church—for many of these refugees are Socialists, Communists, Radicals, Christian Democrats. And since the political tendency in Argentina is moving to the right, here it's quite common for party headquarters and meeting places of other political groups to be bombed. So some members of our church are afraid, and stay at home. But others have continued to support the church, because they see the church is committing itself to real service; and the attendance at our Sunday services has increased.

'But there's another sense in which our congregation is growing. A lot of Chileans have come who have been members of Methodist or other churches, and they come with their questions and problems, and raise questions in the minds of our members that they'd never thought of before!—and it's transformed our congregation. It was a congregation turned in on itself, with a kind of religiosity that was self-centred, subjective, pietistic; but now it's got to think about taking up a more realistic commitment towards the community. And in serving others, it is receiving from others great spiritual benefit—in spite of the fact that life is much more inconvenient, and there are so many problems. Sometimes we're called out at midnight because a refugee has been detained and we have to go to the police, or we have to make a hospital visit—no end of problems! But at the same time, it has been a source of health and renewal for the life of our churches.'

I left Mendoza with a feeling of great affection for this kindly, balanced, tolerant man with long years of pastoral experience who had suddenly found himself caught up in the aftermath of the Chilean political upheaval. Nor was his sober estimate of the dangers of the line he had taken misplaced. Four months after I spoke to him, a bomb explosion in the church destroyed five doors and all the church and manse windows. At the communion service held on the following day, attended by the Catholic Archbishop of Mendoza who came to express his solidarity, Pastor Federico preached on the cost of discipleship, reaffirming his church's decision to go on 'living the gospel in all its demands'.

A few days after I had left Mendoza for Santiago, there was a small earthquake in Chile. The TV news flash reported the epicentre as several hundred miles south of the Chilean capital; mercifully no casualties were sustained, although some people lost their homes. But there was plenty of evidence of the devastation and misery caused by the political earthquake that erupted on September 11, 1973, when jets of the Chilean Air Force bombed the presidential palace—not a difficult target, flanked as it is on two sides by open squares. A few hours later, the body of President Salvador Allende was dragged from the smoking ruins. Now the Moneda Palace has been patched up, and no sign of the attack remains visible from the outside. The scars on the minds and bodies of political prisoners tortured in Pinochet's jails since then will take longer to heal. Manoel is not his real name, since members of his family are still in Chile. I happened to meet him a few days after his release from eighteen months in prison, and before his journey into exile. He described the events that had led up to his ordeal.

His father had died when he was three, and his mother when he was seven. He roamed the streets of Valparaiso, and knew what it was to sleep in a street or a park, to eat the scraps people threw out and to go in for the petty thieving of a child in order to eat.

'When I was twelve, a Methodist pastor found me doing my school homework in a park in Valparaiso, and he took me home. There we talked, and he offered me room in his home, and in effect became my father. He and his wife have since died, but I'm still counted as a brother by his family. In his home, we received a heritage of faith, hope and love which was firmly built into my life. I became a member of the church, and a lay preacher, and it was in the church too that I met my wife.

'But my early experience had brought me very close to the needs of people pushed to the margins of society, deprived of the things they have a right to, and I began to conceive Christianity not as a formula for good habits, but to see the church and the Lord of the church as tremendously relevant and present in the historical life of the people. I've come to understand Christ as the very presence of God who wants to liberate us and bring us the abundant life for which he came. So I have no alternative, in my professional life, in my home, and as a Chilean among my own people, but to witness according to my conscience; and all my preaching action and attitudes are directed towards the real problems that our people feel and have.

'When Allende came to power in 1970, the government invited me to serve in a technical capacity, and I became manager of an engineering concern. Let me say in parenthesis that I knew Allende as a young man, and I can say that he was a really great man, and a great patriot. As a man, he had his faults, like all of us; but if we weigh against his faults his tremendous civic and human virtues, there just isn't any comparison. Allende will be vindicated by history as one of Chile's greatest sons—of this I'm quite certain.'

On September 11, 1973, Manoel was one of the first targets of the military. He was arrested, taken to a prison island off the coast, subjected to barbarous torture (I saw the marks on his body) and made to endure a mock execution. 'I witnessed insults, robbery, the most terrible outrages; but I also experienced how in Christ's name we receive life. On the island, with God's help, we managed to form a church. Here denominations meant nothing—we were simply followers of Christ. We understood that everything that happened to us was the price of our faith; and that if we had to pay such a high price for our faith, then our faith was worth a great deal.

'During the first ten days after the *coup*, many people arrived on the island, among them some foreigners; most were professional people, doctors, engineers, university lecturers, and so on. Among them was a Spanish priest. He was badly maltreated, but retained his integrity. He knew I was a Christian, and on the third Sunday he said to me "What about holding a service?" He spoke with the officer in charge, and after a lot of opposition obtained permission. I preached the word and prayed, he administered the sacrament. It was the most impressive act of worship I've ever attended. This continued for another two Sundays, then he was removed from the island. During my time there I continued to hold Bible studies, later these developed into services, and from this a church grew. But there were many difficulties—it was so crowded, the only place we could meet was a sort of cage— this was our "church", with two men with machine guns on top of it. We had no outside visitor to bring us hope and spiritual help—neither Protestant nor Catholic. But the work of the church continued, and some people were converted. Some people came to understand that in Marxism you've got the scientific instruments for an analysis of social and economic phenomena, but these are not sufficient to feed a man's soul. For this you need faith—you need God.'

Manoel's story—unexpectedly corroborated for me by a quite independent source—may seem odd in the light of the statement put out by leaders of the Chilean Protestant churches in December 1974, hailing the Pinochet regime as the God-given deliverance from Marxism 'through the uprising of the Armed Forces which we recognize as the retaining wall raised by God against atheism'. I spoke with one Baptist pastor who

was a signatory of the document, and he told me that he had
agreed to be present at the meeting with General Pinochet
when the signing took place, on the understanding that he
would have the opportunity of voicing the reserves he had
about the way in which opponents of the regime were being
treated. However, no such opportunity was afforded. Perhaps
he was naïve to have expected it.[6] But he was able to confirm
that the document had originated in the General Secretariat
of the military junta, and that one of the prime movers of the
document was the Rev. Pedro Puentes, who works in the
press section of the Secretariat, and as pastor of the Independent Presbyterian church of Chile, has links with Dr Carl
McIntire's International Council of Christian Churches.
Puentes also made it clear to denominational leaders that
refusal to sign would be interpreted as hostility towards the
junta. You only need to live for a few days in the atmosphere
of fear in Santiago to understand what this means.

In a town in Southern Chile, a Baptist pastor active in
politics was imprisoned, together with a Methodist. Another
Methodist colleague did what he could for him, and then went
to the Baptist leaders. 'Look—your pastor is in prison. Aren't
you going to visit him? Aren't you going to stand by him?'
—'No,' was the reply, 'if we do anything for him, it will be
taken to mean that we agree with what he's done.'

But some Christians have given a courageous witness. A
group of Catholic priests and laymen under Cardinal Raul
Silva have provided a rallying point for victims of the repression. Notable among the Protestants who refused to sign the
document supporting Pinochet was Bishop Helmut Frenz of the
Lutheran church, who has been expelled by the junta for his
determined efforts on behalf of political prisoners and their
families.

When I talked with him in May last year, he had just lost
75 per cent of his church membership, who disapproved of
his work as co-chairman of the Peace Committee. Another
Lutheran pastor had explained to me how the campaign to
oust Frenz had been boosted by the government. 'Now', he

added, 'for the first time I understand how the Nazis manipulated the German churches in the 1930s. I would have found it all incredible—the rigged election of a new church council, presided over by an army officer—if I hadn't seen it with my own eyes.'

Frenz himself, while working for political prisoners and their families, had been careful not to criticize the government publicly—apart from the implied criticism of mass habeas corpus applications at the courts. 'If you publish what I'm telling you now,' he had said with a wry smile, 'you'll find me knocking at the door of your college asking for a job—because they'll throw me out.' Now that he is expelled, and designated by his church to a parish in Hamburg, the only constraint is the communications barrier he feels in trying to share his vision of the suffering people of Chile. 'In Germany,' he says, 'I once asked my parents why they didn't react to the persecution of the Jews. "We didn't know", they replied; but they didn't know because they didn't want to know. Today, we must bear witness of what we have seen, and of what our Lord has done through us—it *must* be made known. You need to see a mother whose daughter, son, husband have been tortured in prison, and you forget to ask the question, "Is she left-wing?"'

We live in an age of terrorism. But torture used by a government as an instrument of policy is the worst form of terror (Huddleston). This was the political atmosphere that Frenz had been enduring in Santiago. Under the cover of the state of siege, still in force nearly three years after the *coup*, the DINA arrest people and engineer their disappearance. 'Nobody knows where they are, and the government denies knowledge of them', he told me. 'But we try to document these cases with eye-witnesses, and make representations at the courts. Secondly, we have been giving assistance to those who have lost their jobs, and students who have been expelled from university, for political reasons. Thirdly, we have been giving financial help for the organization of communal workshops, in an effort to provide employment, especially for

89

released prisoners. Fourthly, we have set up children's canteens in the shanty towns, to assuage the worst effects of malnutrition, which plagues over 30 per cent of children in many areas of Santiago. Also, we try as best we can to help the families of people who have been arrested or made to disappear. In some cases we cannot give practical help, but the fact that they can come and sit here and tell us their problems without fear—this is important pastorally.'

How had Frenz incurred the charges of political bias, not only by the government but from within his own church? To answer this, he outlined the history of the Lutheran church in Chile. 'We started as a church among German-speaking immigrants, and during many years we lived in a ghetto. We preached only in German, we taught in German, all the thinking was German-oriented. But the social and political situation in Chile 50–100 years ago didn't help us. Chilean society built up the walls of the ghetto from the outside, and we did it from the inside.'

But when Frenz came to Chile, he gave a sharp impetus to a movement that was already gathering strength to emphasize the mission of the church to the Chilean people. 'A church doesn't make a mission, it *is* a mission, if I understand the New Testament.' This missionary activity resulted in the formation of Spanish-speaking congregations, composed mainly of people who had taken a personal decision for Christ and had been baptized as adults, in contrast to many in the German-speaking congregation who were members because they were Germans and belonged to a certain social class. This shift in policy caused a tension within the church, which was accentuated by the political history of the last five years. When Allende became president in 1970, the majority of the German members, well-to-do farmers, bankers and merchants, were adversely affected by the policies of the new government. Expropriation of land and industry took place. In this situation, the church leaders, the pastors, the church council, did not react to defend the property of the members, not because they supported Allende, but because there was no request for help—landowners had their own means of looking after their interests. But when the *coup* happened, and the military government began the systematic persecution of all Allende supporters, the church leaders began to denounce the violation of human rights.

'At that moment, it was like a bomb in the church', said Frenz. 'The attitude was: "Look, now the pastors are taking political action. Before, they didn't defend us; but now they defend our enemies." And it was difficult, or rather impossible, to convince people that really there's a big difference between defending property and privilege, and defending the dignity of a human being and his very life.' In spite of the attempts by two leading Lutheran pastors from Germany to mediate, the majority of the German-speaking congregation hived off and formed a new church in protest against Frenz.

'It's very hard for our church now', he told me, 'but I personally feel that what's happening is also very natural. It's the consequence of our consistency, for the essence of Christian faith is to be consistent with the Gospel, not to look for large numbers. I'm aware that the action we are taking now to defend human rights and the dignity of the human being as sons of God can be interpreted as political action—we cannot deny it. But the motivation for our doing this is not an ideology, but the Gospel. We try to do nothing else but to be consistent with the Gospel and to take the place of the good Samaritan.'

But by trying to take the place of the good Samaritan, Frenz has found himself moving politically further and further to the left. 'I started as a naïve liberal Christian', he says; 'I became a highly politicized Christian. I am not a Marxist, nor was I an Allende sympathizer; but I am for liberation. I have found a new vision of the struggle of the poor against oppression. Class struggle is no Marxist propaganda; it is a reality. In Chile, the poor are born poor to die poorer; the rich only get richer.'

This does not mean that Frenz advocates violence. His understanding is that the liberation the gospel teaches must be non-violent, and he echoes Helder Camara's phrase: 'I prefer to be killed than to kill another.' 'But we as Christians cannot be neutral, because our God is not a neutral God. He took sides for humanity, and where humanity is at risk, the Church cannot be neutral. This does not mean we must create a new party; but a Christian cannot be neutral, because he is responsible for peace and justice in the world. A neutral church is an irresponsible church. Jesus challenges us to show how we are contributing to peace and justice. Political neutrality is an illusion, since political abstinence is a veiled way of acting politically. He who backs away from political responsibility becomes a collaborator with tyranny. In such a situation, the church is told to shut up when it criticizes; but when it applauds the government, it is told "this is pure gospel".[7] Political neutrality is a sign that the church is not willing to accept responsibility for the humanity of man.'

Frenz's expulsion from Chile last year was a serious blow to the prophetic role of the church; and the government quickly followed his expulsion by suppressing the Peace Committee of which he was co-chairman. However, Cardinal Raul Silva of Santiago responded immediately by forming a Vicariate of Solidarity, which is carrying on the work of the Committee; and while the Vicariate still exists, victims of the Chilean secret police will still have someone concerned enough to document their case and courageous enough to champion their cause in the face of tyranny and oppression.

CHAPTER FIVE

Between Captivity and Liberation

> When the Christians dare to give a whole-hearted
> revolutionary witness, then the Latin American
> revolution will be invincible.
>
> *Che Guevara*

THEOLOGY of liberation has been defined as 'critical
reflection on Christian action in the light of the Word of
God'. I have tried to illustrate the relation of reflection and
action in this report of encounters with people doing theology
in Latin America—both those whose names are by now well
known, and those who do their theology unnoticed by the
respectable academic journals, which frequently appear to fill
their pages with the modern equivalent of debate about the
number of angels that can dance on the head of a pin. Increasingly, however, one observes a dialogue evolving between
Latin American theology and the established centres of
theological thought around the world. As Miguez Bonino puts
it, 'the theology of liberation is a question addressed to the
Christian obedience of our brethren in Christ elsewhere'.[1] We
cannot evade the question, for it challenges our very understanding of the gospel, and it calls in question the policies and
activities of the agencies involved in theological education,
mission and aid in Latin America. (It may also throw new
light on the role of the churches within our own society; but
to discuss this would need another book.) But even without
these compelling reasons, common courtesy demands attention
to a question posed in a spirit of anxious enquiry; and, bear-
ing in mind the circumstances from which the question arises,
a certain humility is appropriate as we attempt our response.
Segundo's words, quoted at the beginning of this book, are
sufficient reminder that, at the Latin American end of the
dialogue at least, what is involved is no mere theological

93

word-game, but a matter of life and death. As Luther once put it, 'not reading and speculation, but living, dying and being condemned make a real theologian'.[2]

The question posed is perhaps most succinctly articulated by Gustavo Gutierrez. He speaks of the way in which much contemporary theology appears to take as its starting point the challenge of the non-believer. Bonhoeffer's searching question 'How do we speak of God in a world come of age?'— how to express Christian faith in a secular society—set the agenda for a generation of theological thought in Britain, Europe and the U.S.A. But we were too parochial in our vision. Secular theology was too limited, even in the non-religious culture of western society, let alone in areas such as Latin America. Here, as Gutierrez points out, 'the challenge does not come primarily from the non-believer, but from the man who is not a man, who is not recognized as such by the existing social order. He is in the ranks of the poor, the exploited; he is the man who is systematically and legally despoiled of his being as a man; who scarcely knows that he *is* a man. His challenge is not aimed first at our religious world, but at our *economic, social, political and cultural world.* Therefore it is an appeal for the revolutionary transformation of the very bases of a dehumanizing society. *The question therefore is not how to speak of God in an adult world, but how to proclaim him as a Father in a world that is not human. What is implied in telling this man who is not a man that he is a son of God?*'[3] In a sense, the whole of Latin American theology of liberation evolves out of the attempt to explore that one question.

One answer commonly given seeks to evade the implications altogether. The argument runs something like this. Christian faith first appeared in a world of appalling injustice and inequality. When Jesus preached the good news in Galilee, his own people were under the thumb of Roman domination; and when the gospel moved out into the wider world of the Roman Empire, it was proclaimed in a society where two-thirds of the population were slaves without any human rights whatever. Yet never was there any suggestion that the gospel involved incitement to political revolution. On the contrary, Jesus rejected the political interpretation of messiahship current among his Jewish contemporaries, exhorted his fellow-Jews to be subservient to the demands of the Roman military, and taught obedience to imperial authority. Paul echoes the teaching of Jesus in his insistence on payment of taxes, is represented as constantly appealing to the authority of Rome for legal protection, and never so much as hints that slaves (who may well have been in the majority in many of the early Christian congregations) should be other than obedient, willing and loyal to their taskmasters.

There are two main objections to this argument. The first is on the historical level at which it is posited. For it is true, of course, that Jesus never proclaimed political revolution, nor did he support the Zealots actively engaged in fomenting it. Attempts to identify him with the Zealot party are based on fanciful interpretation of evidence, not on careful scholarship.[4] But equally, there is no denying the fact that, to the religio-political power structure of his day, he posed a threat which evoked the inevitable hostile and ruthless reaction; and his condemnation and execution as subversive of public order cannot be watered down to a mere miscarriage of justice without seriously distorting the facts. 'By regarding him as a Zealot rebel, Pilate certainly misunderstood Jesus, and because of his fear of a popular revolt was bound so to misunderstand him. But in the deeper sense of a challenge to the Pax Romana and its gods and laws, we can look back and realize that Pilate understood him aright. This is shown by the effect that the crucified man from Nazareth ultimately had upon the Roman Empire in the life of early Christianity. The worship of such a "crucified God" contained a strictly political significance which cannot be sublimated into the religious sphere.'[5] The fact that Jesus was no Zealot fomentor of armed rebellion cannot be allowed to obscure the political implications of his concern for the liberation of the oppressed,[6] nor are we at liberty to spiritualize the meaning of this concern out of existence.

But a more fundamental objection is to observe that in fact there is no short-cut from the political stance of Jesus in the first century—however it is evaluated—to Christian obedience in the political realities of the twentieth century. 'Discipleship is not doing over again what Jesus did. It is freely living by what he did' (F. Herzog). A simplistic 'imitation of Christ' approach to the problem is hopelessly naïve,[7] since it fails to recognize both the uniqueness of the historical mission of Jesus, and the incarnation as the beginning of a historical process of liberation, which would inevitably evolve in increasingly complex manifestations. 'The life and preaching of Jesus postulate the increasing search for a new kind of man in a qualitatively different society. Although the Kingdom must not be confused with the establishment of a just society, this does not mean that it is indifferent to this society.... To preach the universal love of the Father is inevitably to go against all injustice, privilege, oppression, or narrow nationalism.'[8] If this be so, the Christian in the twentieth century is not exempt from a search for and support of the political options which will help to bring this about.[9]

Thus far, a considerable measure of agreement among Christians might be registered. Many are ready to applaud when theologians of liberation denounce injustice and oppression, expose the institutionalized violence that condemns millions to a life of misery in sub-human conditions, encourage the dispossessed in their growing awareness of the socio-political realities in which they live, and challenge Christians consciously to opt for the poor and exploited and to work for social change.[10] The parting of the ways occurs at the point where the question is asked: 'Which political options?' And the uneasiness turns to alarm as it becomes increasingly clear that the instrument favoured for a socio-political analysis and a guide for action is Marxism.[11]

Thus, for example, in his London lectures on Christians and Marxists, Dr Miguez Bonino assumes, as one of his basic presuppositions, 'that the socio-analytical tools, the historical horizon of interpretation, the insight into the dynamics of the social process and the revolutionary ethos and programme which Marxism has either received and appropriated or itself created are, however, corrected or reinterpreted, indispensable for revolutionary change.'[12] Or again, Aharon Sapsezian tells of a visit to a theological school in Santiago where he was shown the description of a project on Christian-Marxist studies. Having glanced at the list of possible participants, he enquired which of them were Christians and which of them Marxists. 'They are all Marxist Christians', was the reply. 'One wonders', he comments, 'how this is possible without some kind of schizophrenic hang-up or without seriously blurring one's identity. Yet the hard fact remains that many Christians have found it not only possible, but enriching, to use categories of social analysis and political theory (amongst which Marxist categories are inevitable) in discerning new dimensions of their faith and service.'[13]

This is no place to enter into a lengthy discussion on Christian-Marxist dialogue, on which a considerable literature already exists.[14] But some appraisal of the criticisms levelled against the Marxism of Latin American theologians is appropriate at this point.

1. The charge is commonly made that Latin Americans display an uncritical acceptance of Marxism as *the* scientific tool for analysing the social and economic malaise of Latin America. R. H. Preston claims that Gutierrez assumes he has found in Marxism a scientific approach in order to discover laws proper to the political world which will give revolutionary activity effectiveness.[15] J. Moltmann implies that the Latin Americans simply make declamations of 'seminar-Marxism' as a world view that is out of touch with the working and suffering people.[16] Stephen Neill accuses Miguez Bonino of accepting the Marxist analysis of society 'hook, line and sinker'.[17]

These are astonishing charges to anyone who has experienced the reality that has given birth to Latin American theology. The 'radical turn toward the people' that Moltmann calls for has already taken place; without this, there would be no theology of liberation. It is precisely in this close contact with the people that terms like 'class struggle', 'exploitation', 'alienation', are seen for what they are: not mere words in a treatise on sociology or economics, nor the discoveries of Karl Marx at his reading desk in the British Museum, but the realities that stand up and hit you in the favelas and barriadas of every Latin American city, in the plantations and estates of the Latin American countryside. What Marx has done is to help Christians in these countries make sense of their world, and suggest guidelines to change it; but no Latin American in his senses would accept Marxist analysis in its original form and detail, arising as it did from the experiences of Britain and Europe in the nineteenth century. Segundo, for instance, makes it clear that 'it would make no sense to cling doggedly to Marx when he himself never claimed that his views were worth more than the arguments on which they were based, and when we realize that his arguments were applicable to revolutionary conditions existing in an epoch very different from our own'.[18]

Bonino, having stated his belief in the validity of the Marxist heritage, '*however corrected or reinterpreted*' (my italics), goes on to devote a book to a critical examination of the relation between Christian faith and Marxism. We cannot here summarize his argument. It is enough at this point to refer to his own summary[19] of Camilo Torres' analysis of Christian love, economic planning, and class struggle, in his paper: 'Revolution: Christian Imperative'.[20] Torres' orientation is Marxist, but critically so, and adapted to the concrete situation in Latin America, as anyone who has lived there will immediately recognize; and Bonino's summary is the starting point for the most comprehensive critique to date of Christian-Marxist dialogue from a Latin American perspective.

Rubem Alves, while declaring that it is impossible to ignore the great contribution Marxist method makes to our understanding of reality, goes on to point out that no method,

Marxist included, is devoid of presupposition; and that the presupposition behind Marxist method is that the essence of society is economy. 'The question of values and the qualitative dimensions of life are ignored. They cannot be dealt with statistically, ergo, they are not an object of scientific knowledge. Capitalists and Marxists share the same outlook, seeing the world through the economic perspective. They are cooks who are in basic agreement as to the ingredients to be used, quarrelling only about how to mix them.'[21]

Helder Camara bases his criticism of Marxism on its track record in countries with Marxist governments. He would agree with Torres' assessment of their achievement in a juster distribution of wealth and an astonishing industrial development; but he asks 'how Marxism can be humanistic or liberating, when in Marxist-dominated countries, those who will not accept scientific materialism are repudiated and marginalized, and the human person thwarted? Moreover, have not the Marxist super powers become empires, just as much as the capitalist super powers? Either bloc is quite willing to take advantage of the other's moments of internal dissension, and both together will cynically make common cause whenever that would seem to serve their common interests.'[22]

These quotations may be taken as representative of the fact that (*pace* Preston, Neill, *et al*) Latin American theology does not swallow Marxism uncritically; and the relationships I have described in the previous chapters should be sufficient to challenge the assumption that this theology espouses a theoretical Marxism divorced from the grass-roots realities of the Latin American people in their struggle for liberation.

2. Another criticism of the Latin Americans is that their theology is hopelessly Utopian, and out of touch with the realities of power and politics in the modern world.[23] This leads, on the one hand, to 'the despising of precise goals and the presentation of impossibilities as possibilities'; and on the other, to a dangerous identification of the Kingdom of God with a political cause, the absolutizing of revolution and 'the

atmosphere of holy wars'.[24] P. Hebblethwaite remarks that 'a revolutionary who claims to have God on his side is more fearsome, because more self-righteous, than a revolutionary armed merely with a sten-gun'; and he goes on to attack Gutierrez' rejection of dualism as the reverse of liberating, since it was the process of secularization which 'delivered the Church from the extravagant and ultimately damaging claim to be able to intervene anywhere'.[25]

It seems to me that these criticisms miss the point even more completely. In the first place, Gutierrez insists that the concept of Utopia must be related to present possibilities. 'If Utopia does not lead to action in the present, it is an evasion of reality.' And he goes on to quote Ricoeur's assertion that 'Utopia is deceiving when it is not concretely related to the possibilities offered to each era'.[26] Peter Hughes was simply invoking this concept of Utopian denunciation and annunciation when he encouraged the people of Vila Maria to mobilize themselves for very specific goals and objectives.[27] There is not much Utopianism, in the pejorative sense of unreality, when a local community demand to be included in the city's garbage disposal service! Utopianism, so understood, is not some pipe dream of an impossibly perfect society, but, as Alves points out, it is first 'the belief in the non-necessity of *this* imperfect order'—a lesson, he implies, that advocates of 'Christian realism' like Sanders ought to have learnt since the days of Watergate, the Pentagon Papers and the falsification of bombing reports.[28]

Moreover, when Gutierrez argues for a monist view of the work of Christ in the world, at no point does he identify the Kingdom of God with an ecclesiastical institution, a political party, or a revolutionary movement. In his careful exposition of the concept of Utopia[29] he states categorically that there must be no identification of the Kingdom with any particular historical stage of the struggle for liberation. In view of the misconceptions cited above, it may be worth quoting Gutierrez at length on this point:

'Faith proclaims that the brotherhood which is sought

through the abolition of the exploitation of man by man is something possible, that efforts to bring it about are not in vain, that God calls us to it and assures us of its complete fulfilment, and that the definitive reality is being built on what is transitory. Faith reveals to us the deep meaning of the history which we fashion with our own hands: it teaches us that every human act which is oriented towards the construction of a more just society has value in terms of communion with God—in terms of Salvation; inversely it teaches that all injustice is a breach with him.' This, then, is the true meaning of the rejection of dualism. Latin American theologians are not attempting to blur the distinction between church and state (Helder Camara could hardly be accused of this!) nor are they attempting to recover for the church the ground lost in the process of secularization. On the contrary, it is this very process of secularization that has helped some of them to see the unity, not of church and state, *but of God and the world that he has made*, and the unity of history as the one sphere of the redemptive activity of Christ and his Spirit.[30]

This means, on the one hand, a refusal to identify faith with politics. Gutierrez is very specific at this point. 'Christian hope opens us, in an attitude of spiritual childhood, to the gift of the future promised by God. It keeps us from any confusion of the Kingdom with any one historical stage, from any idolatry toward unavoidably ambiguous human achievement, *from any absolutising of revolution*' (my italics). But, and this is equally important, this does not absolve the Christian from the necessity of taking sides, of bridging the gap between faith and politics. 'The mediation of the historical task of the creation of a new man assumes that liberation from sin and communion with God in solidarity with all men —manifested in political liberation and enriched by its contribution—does not fall into idealism and evasion.' Miguez is equally specific on these two poles of the discussion. 'It is indeed necessary to reject as strongly as possible any sacralization of ideology and system... there must be no room for theocratic dreams of any sort from either right or left. But it is important to stress that such a secularization of politics is to be attained not through a new idealism of Christian theology, but through a clear and coherent recognition of historical, analytical and ideological mediations. There is no *divine* politics or economics. But this means that we must resolutely use the best *human* politics and economics at our disposal.'[31]

3. This brings us to the complex problem of the relation between faith and ideology. Once again, a detailed discussion of this relationship would take us far beyond the scope of this book; but since the charge is frequently made that in theology of liberation the gospel has been made captive to Marxist ideology, some treatment of the problem, however brief, is called for. Bonino, for example, quotes the Peruvian Pedro Arana: 'In the ideology of ISAL, God is translated by revolution; the people of God by the revolutionary hosts, and the word of God by the revolutionary writings. Nobody will fail to see that all of this is Marxist humanism.'[32] This charge of ideological captivity is echoed in the response of much European and North American theology.

The reply of the Latin Americans can be summarized in a simple question: 'To what ideology is your gospel a prisoner?' The assumption is often made, perhaps unconsciously, that the traditional theology of the West is somehow pure, neutral and sterilized against any possibility of infection from ideologies.[33] In fact, Western theology has all too frequently been wedded to an ideology of the *status quo*, and lent its tacit support to unjust and oppressive regimes. Nor is this simply a matter of history, but a feature of our contemporary world, as a moment's reflection on the relationship between the Dutch Reformed Church and apartheid (to quote the most obvious example) will indicate. But this is by no means the only expression of theology captive to ideology in modern society.[34] Indeed, the question may well be raised whether it is possible entirely to 'de-ideologize' the gospel any more than ultimately we can demythologize it. Assmann argues that it is impossible to go straight to the heart of Christianity, because Christianity exists only in a series of historical embodiments.[35] Segundo makes much the same point when he writes: 'Even though endowed with absolute value, the Christian faith totally lacks any precise instrument for measuring the historical life of Christians by pre-established standards... Christians cannot evade the necessity of inserting something to fill the void between their faith and their options in history. In short, they cannot avoid the risk of ideologies.'[36]

This may appear unacceptable to those for whom 'ideology' is a pejorative term—as it clearly is, for instance, to the writers of *Commitment without Ideology*. Their concept of ideology is of an overview of reality which stereotypes and oversimplifies, prevents honest communication, and becomes the standard of truth to which experience must conform. 'One's ideology, his most deeply held truth and concern, thus becomes his greatest oppressor.'[37]

But an ideology need not involve delivering one's faith bound and shackled to some monstrous juggernaut. Like it or not, we are bound to interpret our faith through the medium of a view of the world and of history which will give focus to obedience and action. Commitment without ideology may prove to be a mirage, as even its protagonists appear to admit at the end of their discussion. 'Many uncertainties remain. Chief among them will be the question of whether our definition of ideology is sufficiently sharp as not to be open to the charge of a new ideology.'[38] It may be more realistic to face up to the truth in Segundo's view cited above, and accept the risk involved in a critical commitment to ideology as the medium for making faith effective in history.[39] But the operative word here is 'critical'. For example, Christians need to bring a discriminating mind to bear on the political ideologies of both capitalism and socialism, recognizing that differences of opinion will arise over these and other options. But in Bonino's view, the character of the criticism is bound to be different. With capitalism, our Christian commitment should mean that we bring under sharp security the aims and goals of the system and ask whether it is not essentially egotistical, self-seeking and destructive. In the case of socialism, we should recognize that it offers the possibility of a more unselfish, humane and just society—and bring to it the bar of judgement sharply at every point at which it fails to fulfil the aims and objectives which it sets itself.[40]

4. This is a convenient point to face the criticism frequently heard that the espousal of Marxism, if followed to its logical conclusion, would support the movement to implant a totalitarian form of government in the whole sub-continent. It is an objection generally voiced by the comfortable, who are blind to the fact that for millions of their fellow human beings, the only freedom they effectively possess is the freedom to starve, and that the totalitarian nature of the present regimes of most Latin American countries is shown up for what it is the moment anyone raises his voice on behalf of the exploited or in defence of human rights. President Geisel of Brazil put this point recently with a burst of refreshing candour: 'There cannot be a democratic regime where there are shanty towns and people starving to death.'[41]

Cuba is also run by a military dictatorship, and personal freedom is held sharply in check within the bounds set by the regime; but that may not be an exorbitant price to pay for the eradication of starvation, homelessness and unemployment. As Ian Fraser remarks, 'It is hard to envisage any other way in which a quite different set of priorities could be established, so that a gangster's paradise, a country of gamblers and prostitutes, of unemployment and disinheritance of the people, could become a country of genuine basic justice, equality and opportunity. . . . Yes, everyone should have access to justice —but that is no use to him if he does not have enough to eat: survival is more fundamental than justice. Yes, there should be freedom of the press—but what of the vast number of the world's population who cannot read or write?—literacy is a more fundamental right. Yes, there should be development of a country's resources—but what use is that if the benefits are extracted by the rich countries to add to the gap which separates them from the poor ones?'[42] In Cuba, whatever we may think of the political restraints needed to establish these priorities, in twenty years housing, health and education have become the norm for the mass of the population rather than the exception; and more recently new forms of political participation by the majority of people are being evolved.

The Cuban experience is an indication of the fact that Marxist political theory need not produce the excesses of tyrannical rule that exist in the Soviet Union, and that a brand of Latin American socialism may emerge with a more human face than has so far appeared in the Eastern bloc. One of the features of this human face is to be seen in the relationship that is developing between the regime and the Christian churches in Cuba. At first, the revolution had a shattering effect on the churches. But when they began to pick up the pieces, some Christians realized that the revolution had achieved what the churches had been talking about for years —a more just and human life for the majority. From the government's side, recognition of the importance of Christian participation in the revolutionary process has come from Castro himself: 'During the last years, revolutionary trends have been appearing among the Christians in Latin America . . . there is a greater number of priests and religious people who take a definite stand in favour of the process of liberation . . . some are persecuted, others have died, like Camilo Torres. In fact, if we analyse things objectively . . . we must appreciate in its full value the importance of this awakening of a political consciousness of large masses of Christians in this continent. . . .'[43] It is important to observe that this relationship of mutually critical tolerance between the government and the churches exists in a situation where the regime is secure enough to dispense with any alliance with the churches for purely tactical reasons, and suggests an attitude towards religion that stands in marked contrast to that displayed by the Soviet authorities. Camilo Torres, writing in 1964, foresaw how Marxist theory would evolve and outgrow antireligious tactics once it had been shown that religion need not be the opium of the people. While acknowledging the risk of serving as 'useful idiots', Torres advocated the collaboration of Christians with Marxists 'at the level of action where the scope and the doctrinal implications can be limited' in order to participate eventually in the building of a better world.[44] On any showing, the features of a human face of socialism stand a far better chance of emerging than if Christians try to remain aloof from the revolutionary process. In particular, Biblical eschatology will help to check the absolutizing of revolution, putting it in its proper context of the hope of the final coming of the Kingdom; and the Christian view of man will militate against the identification of one's own cause with God's, or the enemy's cause with the devil's. As Bonino puts it, 'no human group or class can be made the exclusive and definitive bearer of evil in history. Evil is a solidary and total responsibility of mankind, and if it is true that it finds historical embodiment within specific conditions and that a class or notion can be the typical and dominant representative of it at a certain point in history, it is also true that it cannot erase the power of the risen Christ present in all humanity, nor excuse our own responsibility for all of mankind.'[45]

Hence, while a good deal of the criticism commonly levelled against the Latin Americans can be refuted from a more careful reading of their own writings, no one would pretend that this alliance of Christian theology and Marxist ideology is without its dangers; indeed, Latin American theologians are as aware of the dangers as any of their critics.[46] But provided this awareness can be maintained and sharpened, the indications are that the dialectic between critical reflection on the one hand, and determined action at the grass-roots level on the other, will prove theology of liberation to be a genuinely liberating force in Latin America. It will, however, need to convince some of its most hostile critics within the sub-continent itself.

For it would be a mistake to imagine that theology of liberation is the 'in thing' in Latin America. Allowing for certain outstanding exceptions, the theology taught in most Latin American seminaries and Bible schools is of a conservative and traditional nature, and the teaching methods used indicate a heavy reliance on what Paulo Freire describes as the banking concept of education[47]—the depositing of sums of knowledge with the pupil, the accumulation of which the teacher occasionally tests by 'cashing a cheque' in the form of a written examination. This, says Freire, is education for domestication, not liberation. An example of this approach is to be seen in one of the publications of a Brazilian Protestant seminary, as part of a course of programmed learning intended for laymen studying at home and meeting periodically with a tutor and fellow students. At certain points in the course, a student is encouraged to give an answer in his own words, but on the whole the questions are in the form of sentences left with a blank which the student has to fill in with a single word answer. In this particular volume, an introduction to the life of Christ, there is a section on the social dimension of the Gospel, and the student is invited to respond by indicating the 'right' answer.

'There will be peace and social justice among men when . . . (now underline the best answer):
   (a) When all men are baptized in an evangelical (i.e. Protestant) church;
   (b) When the great powers stop making bombs and arms;
   (c) When men obey the will of God;
   (d) When all the money of the rich is divided among the poor.'

The lesson continues 'When all men obey God's will, they will have solved their spiritual problems. And as a result, they will also solve their . . . [here the student is expected to write 'material' or 'social'] problems. It is not a sin to be rich, nor a virtue to be poor. We are stewards of our money. Money is only the occasion of sin when we love it more than God. The best things in life cannot be bought with money.' All this from an institution where teachers would view with alarm the suggestion of the ideological manipulation of Christian faith. And although the example given is at a very unsophisticated level, it is reflection of the methods and ethos of a good deal that goes on in the seminaries at a much more advanced level of study.

But among the minority of teachers who believe that one of the chief aims of theological education should be to foster a critical awareness, some still feel that there is a place for the seminary as an institution. ISEDET in Buenos Aires, the result of a merger in 1970 between the Lutheran and Union (largely Methodist and Presbyterian) seminaries, has in its stated aims a passage worth quoting:

'Both our experience and theological reflection indicate to us the importance of a profound relationship between our particular Latin American history and faithfulness to the Gospel, a faithfulness which must be expressed in the indissoluble unity of action and thought.

'Thus we see ourselves obligated to define more exactly the context in which we live. The Latin America to which we belong is a continent of dependence, neocolonialism, exploitation and misery. It is also a continent where the long presence of Christian churches has left indelible marks which are at the same time reason for repentance as well as for hope among Christians. And Latin America is a continent—and perhaps this is most important—where there is emerging a growing eagerness for liberation and where there is struggle against oppression and for the creation of a new society and the manifestation of a new form of existence, of new men jointly responsible for and determining their own history.

'What happens when we reflect on the Gospel and try to live it in this context? What stands out is that intimate relationship between the liberating message of the Kingdom and our situation. The Gospel denounces sin, illuminates hope, and calls into being the task of total liberation. Our context impels us, as a result, to make our faithfulness to Jesus Christ more profound, more alive and more efficacious.

'We perceive at the same time the ambiguity of our tradition, our heritage, and our conduct and thought as Christians. We also see ourselves as part of an unjust system and a fallen society, as well as part of the thought and practice which justify oppression. This double awareness—both of the pertinence and the ambiguity of the Christian faith in Latin America —leads us to the necessity of a critical revision and modernizing of the Christian message, thought, and action. *We believe that this is the heart of our profession as professors of theology.*'[48]

Others, however, equally committed to this view of the role of theology, believe that institutionalized theological education is essentially incompatible with theology of liberation, whose proper context is the life and struggle of the people. Take it out of this context, give it professional status, and it would be in danger of losing its essential being. Hence the reluctance, even of its ablest exponents, to allow it to become a new 'consumer good'[49] in the theological market, or to give it priority over a single act of solidarity which will help men achieve a genuinely human life.[50] So they are beginning to experiment with other ways of learning. In Peru, a group of theological students spent a year of their course in an 'immersion experience', living for three months in turn with slum dwellers in Lima, coastal fishermen and Andean peasants. Luis Reinoso, secretary of Celadec (the Latin American Evangelical Council for Christian Education), described this last experience.

'The students lived in an Indian community up in the Andes. They chose the community themselves—one without any church, Protestant or Catholic—the nearest Catholic church was some miles away. The students said nothing about their being Christians—they simply introduced themselves as students who wanted to share the peasants' life. So they started by getting up at 4 a.m., and by 5 a.m. they were out on the land. At 6 they had breakfast, which was a cup of herb tea— no bread! Then they continued ploughing the land, and conversation would go on about their concerns: a crop lost through disease, the variations in market prices for their produce, what they would earn in a month, and so on. Lunch would last for half an hour, and then they would work through until 4 p.m. After many days of this, the students had a new insight into the ideas, the life, the work, the needs, the hopes of these peasants. And they discovered that much of what they had learnt in the seminary was of little or no use; and they began to wonder if the kind of institutional church we have is relevant to the daily life and the community needs of these people.' As Reinoso sees it, the first prerequisite for a theological student is to learn from the people before he tries to teach them anything, and *then* to attempt to reflect on his experience in the light of his faith. It is the expression in theological education of Freire's concept of conscientization.[51]

These experiments do not imply a complete abandonment of the traditional theological institutions and disciplines. But they do imply a far more questioning attitude to theological method. And one reason for the popularity of Marx among Latin American theologians is that, along with Freud, he is regarded as one of the masters of the art of 'suspecting'. Besides a critical interpretation of the Bible, there is need for a critical interpretation of reality, for which psychology and sociology provide some of the necessary instruments. According to Segundo, we need to encourage theological students not only to understand the Bible in depth; we must enable them to undertake a profounder reading of the newspapers and other media of communication. This would be a significant contribution towards the liberation of theology, without which there can be no theology of liberation.

Another important contribution to bringing theology out of the seminary is the dissemination throughout Latin America of the CELADEC course of study entitled 'New Life in Christ'. Since its inception in 1962, this graded curriculum for Sunday Schools has become increasingly radicalized, and in its later phases makes quite explicit comparisons between the oppression suffered by the people of Israel and that endured by the Latin American masses,[52] illustrating the struggle for justice not only from Biblical material, but also from anecdotes of contemporary Latin American life. This course, in the hands of groups of lay people, could also become an effective instrument for a greater awareness of their own potential to initiate change.

One consequence of this growing awareness among Christians is the realization of the ambiguous role of Christian mission in their own countries. This has penetrated to some mission boards in Britain and the U.S.A. And missionaries are beginning to ask themselves whether their presence helps to prolong an enterprise involved in the conditions of injustice and dependence that they live amongst, or whether their activities are an ally in the struggle for liberation. In the minds of many, the image of a church with foreign priests and pastors is of a church associated with imperialism; and the call for a missionary moratorium has been heard.[53] But with few exceptions, I did not find theologians and church leaders in favour of it. To them, it was not a question of 'foreignness', but of the attitude of the missionary, national or expatriate. Gutierrez pays tribute to certain foreign missionaries who, although not born in Latin America, understand the situation better than some of those who were and who by their exploitation of their own people seem more foreign than the foreigners. The consensus of opinion seems to be that, while at present the proportion of expatriate leaders is still too high, making for distortion in the Latin American churches and inhibiting the discovery of indigenous resources, there is still room for those who will come prepared to make a conscious commitment to the marginalized people of the Continent. This implies acceptance of the poor as an exploited social class, together with a clear political awareness of the social reality in which the poor live, and becoming identified with their struggle in an effective way—a different matter from working among the poor as an agent of those churches in the rich world who ease their conscience by sending money and powdered milk with the gospel. This has obvious implications for agencies such as Oxfam and Christian Aid, as well as for missionary societies; on the whole, my observation of projects supported by these agencies suggests a far clearer grasp of the actual sociological function and direction of their work than is sometimes the case with the work of mission boards. There is no such thing as preaching the gospel to people in a vacuum; we must take more seriously into account the economic, political and cultural factors that surround these people, and the concrete results of our work not just with individuals but in the life of society. It is therefore like water in the desert to come across this statement of policy by one North American Board of Missions:

'Jesus was appointed to preach the Good News to the poor, proclaim liberty to the captives, give sight to the blind, set free the oppressed, and proclaim the acceptable year of the Lord. The Board of Missions agrees with many Latin American churches that mission today has as its fundamental task proclaiming Christ's gospel, initiating and supporting movements for greater social justice, working towards the liberation of oppressed people, and trying to create alternatives to racism and exploitation.... As the board broadens its understanding of God's mission to include the transforming of social systems, increasingly it will be judging programs and policy in the light of their impact upon the struggle for justice in the world.'[54]

'The struggle for justice...' is a high-sounding phrase. Behind it, there still lurk at least two questions that need to be faced. One is the question by what right we in the affluent countries presume to bring any message of social salvation as an integral part of our Christian message, to the poor of the Third World, as if we ourselves have found the key to a truly human way of life. On the contrary, our affluent, consumer society may be just as inhuman in its own way, perhaps even more so. Perhaps the boot is on the other foot, and salvation will come to us from the poor,[55] who have learned to live with less material comfort and possessions, who live a happier life because they are less greedy, and who by their life style demonstrate a greater respect for the earth's limited resources and possessions, thus pointing the way for the whole of humanity if civilized life is to survive on this planet. There is, of course, an element of truth in this; but let us be clear that in Latin America we are dealing not just with poverty but with misery even more destructive of the possibilities of a genuinely human life than the unbridled materialism of our own society. There is something nauseating about lofty assurances from the comfortable that the poor are happy and we ought not to foist our standard of living on them. That so much human sympathy and love, so much cheerfulness and courage is to be found in the shanty towns and rural slums of Brazil and Peru is a tribute to the human spirit which emerges triumphant in spite of the hunger, disease, squalor and deprivation which is its constant habitat;[56] but that is no reason to condone the institutionalized violence that deprives the majority of the population of the basic essentials for human life, such as sanitation, housing, health, education, employment, food, *and a say in running their lives.*

But secondly, what form is the struggle for justice to take? Christians who refuse to allow the affluent decadence of our own society to blind them to the revolution of the gospel would in principle applaud the words of Che Guevara quoted at the heading of this chapter—if only they had not been uttered by a Marxist guerrilla who met his death leading an armed rebellion. Revolution too often connotes violence. But revolutionary violence, even if it can be justified as a lesser evil than the repressive violence of military regimes,[57] only provokes a yet greater reactionary violence in the endless 'spiral of violence'[58] that Camara envisages as the sterile result of armed insurrection. The American trained Bolivian army rangers who hunted out and killed Guevara have their efficient counterparts in almost every country south of the Rio Grande; since Castro entered Havana in triumph, Washington is determined that there shall be no more Cubas in its own backyard. Where economic subversion—as in Chile—fails to overthrow socialist leadership, more direct means will be employed. Dennis Bloodworth, writing in *The Observer* the Sunday after the death of Mao Tse Tung, said of him: 'Crude though he could be himself, he taught the whole world manners. For it is to be wondered just how much less consideration the affluent would be paying to the indigent today without that new Maoist dimension which gives perspective and reality to the threat of revolution.'[59] He was too sweeping; the only lesson learned from Mao by the Latin American military, and their Pentagon advisers, is to ensure that, since power grows out of the barrel of a gun, their own finger will stay firmly on the trigger.

But hope remains, even in captivity. We have yet to witness the cumulative effect of the grass-roots communities where independence of spirit is awakened, where hope is kept alive and courage nourished, where protest is expressed in songs which expose tyranny to laughter and derision, where love is demonstrated in a passionate moral force for change that stops short only of physical violence, and where faith is kindled in the power of God who puts down the mighty from their seats, and exalts the humble and meek. Nor is the message of the unknown prophet of the exile forgotten, whose stirring summons to a people in exile to hope against hope is recorded in Isaiah 40:1 f. This side of the resurrection, Paul speaks of the hope that must characterize the church, in the context of his vision of the whole of creation freed from bondage and possessing the liberty of the sons of God (Rom. 8:18 f.). But it is not just a question of hope. One of the things the Christian shares with the Marxist is a view of history which is at once an assurance of the 'good time coming' *and* a summons to pour his energy, love and devotion into the stream of events that will eventually lead to the fulfilment of his hopes.[60] Although the end may be conceived differently, the vision of both Christian and Marxist converge at significant points; and the Marxist too has his version of hoping against hope that spurs him to action. 'Anyone who talks about a model of society that has to be created is invariably treated as a Utopian. That is how . . . the bourgeoisie thought before the October revolution: "It has never been seen; it exists nowhere. Therefore, it is impossible." ' The revolutionaries surprised such forecasts. 'They did not know it was impossible, so they did it.'[61]

At present it seems impossible to resolve the contradiction

that Latin America is a region of untold natural wealth and untold human misery. But it is also a region unique in the Third World, in that the majority of its peoples owe at least a nominal allegiance to Christianity, while millions would confess a positive faith and commitment. When to this is added an awareness of the revolutionary meaning of that faith, and Christians begin to lose their time-honoured addiction to existing authority, and become identified with the 'suppliants of history' (Lehmann), they too will surprise such forecasts and achieve the impossible.

NOTES

INTRODUCTION

(The number after an author's name refers to the numbered bibliography)

1 For an enlightening account of CIA activity involved in the *coup*, see Agee, 1, pp. 361 f.
2 Cf. Moltmann, 62, p. 8
3 Bonino, 10, p. 4
4 Bonino, 10, p. 7
5 Quoted in Bonino, 10, p. 8
6 Bonino, 11, p. 16
7 i.e. Argentina, Bolivia, Brazil, Chile, Ecuador, Paraguay, Peru and Uruguay.
Peru has a population of 16 million. Its president, Gen Francesco Morales Bermundez, seized power in August 1975 from General Juan Velasco Alvarado, who led the military *coup* in 1968. Since July 1976 constitutional guarantees have been suspended, and government policies have moved further to the right.
Bolivia has 5 million people, and is one of the most feudal societies in Latin America. General Hugo Banzer took power in a *coup* in 1971 and declared a state of emergency in 1975, banning political parties and suppressing trade unions.
Brazil is the giant of Latin America, with a population of 110 million, and aspires to be the United States of the future. Its President, General Ernesto Geisel, is the fourth general to serve as head of state since the *coup* in 1964. He is reputed to advocate a return to a more liberal regime, but to date appears unable to convince the hard-liners in his government.
Uruguay, with a population of 3 million, is the most European of the South American states. The army took control in 1973 in the wake of the Tupamaro urban guerrilla movement. The present head of state is President Aparicio Mendes, who took office in 1976.
Argentina, with 25 million, fell under military control in March 1976, when General Jorge Videla ousted Maria Estela Peron from the presidency. The incidence of political assassination continues to be the highest in Latin America.

Chile has a population of 11 million and appeared to have the most stable democracy in Latin America. Since the 1973 *coup* which overthrew the Marxist president Allende and brought General Augusto Pinochet to power, his government has become notorious for the most ruthless political repression in the sub-continent. In November 1976, 322 political prisoners were released, but twice this number are still held, while hundreds arrested by DINA, the secret police, are still not accounted for

8 For an excellent 'bird's eye view', see Castro, 18

CHAPTER ONE

1 Cox, 21, p. 193
2 Gutierrez, 45, p. 295
3 Gutierrez, 45, p. 301
4 Gutierrez, 45, p. 37
5 Gutierrez, 45, p. 177
6 Gutierrez, 45, p. 138
7 Bonino, 10, p. 16
8 Gutierrez, 8 (introduction), p. 12
9 Cf. Illich's blistering attack, 'The seamy side of charity' in 47, pp. 47 f.
10 Cf. Gutierrez, 45, p. 265
11 Bonino, 10, p. 6

CHAPTER TWO

1 Paz, 30, p. 21
2 Cf. p. 45 and p. 107
3 One expression of the move towards indigenization was Arias' own resignation as bishop a year later. Since the Aymara-speaking people account for half the total Methodist membership of 4,000 in Bolivia, it was inevitable that sooner or later a national leader who could speak Aymara take over as Bishop. Arias has asked for a pastorate in the altiplano mining town of Oruru, where he hopes to work among the miners
4 Castro, 18, p. 91
5 'La Massacre del Valle, Cuadernos Justicia y Paz', La Paz, 1975

CHAPTER THREE

1 Cf. Julio de Santa Ana, 68, pp. 188–97
2 Alves, 2

3 Alves, 3
4 The widespread use of arbitrary arrest and torture is well documented by Bruneau, 14, pp. 179–216
5 Lehmann, 54, p. 101 and *passim*, 55, p. xi and *passim*
6 Alves, 3, p. 204
7 Cf. the judgement of another Protestant theologian: 'The time is quickly drawing upon the people of God in Latin America, indeed it is already here, when neither Catholics nor Protestants will be able to bear an effective witness for Christ except as Christians.' Costas, 20, p. 355
8 Although the Recife police did just that with Methodist missionary Fred Morris. For a graphic account of his arrest and torture as a result of his contact with Dom Helder, see *New Internationalist*, January 1977, pp. 20–1
9 Documented in Gheerbrant, 42, pp. 121 f,; *Between Honesty and Hope*, 65, pp. 171 f.
10 It would be a mistake to regard Dom Helder's conflict with the Brazilian authorities as an isolated affair. For a well-documented analysis of the growing confrontation between church and state in Brazil, see Bruneau, 14. Cf. the National Conference of Brazilian Bishops document 'A Pastoral Letter to the People of God', November 16, 1976, of which the following is an extract:

'Violence breeds violence. Violence against political prisoners is committed by soldiers and police. The perversion of the police force is obvious. Recent attacks are classified as terrorist organization activity on the Latin American continent. One manifestation of military political terrorism on the continent was the arrest of 17 Catholic bishops in Riobamba, Ecuador, on August 13.

Who should be blamed for the wave of perversity which has grown to alarming proportions? Or, what is behind all the crimes in our country which have reached a degree of refined cruelty?

The pernicious and ominous practice of labeling bishops, priests and laypeople as subversives and agitators, when they defend poor and humble people, prisoners and victims of torture, contributes to crime, violence and highhandedness. In view of the incidents, which are shocking to public opinion, we cannot blame just the low-ranking policemen who pulls the trigger of the revolver or this or that policeman or soldier.

We must search for the underlying causes which act together to create a climate of violence. Among the principal causes of violence we stipulate the following:

The poor are deprived of justice; poor people are defenseless; they fill the jails, where torture is frequent; they are imprisoned on charges of not carrying identification papers or taken under arrest in police dragnet raids; only the poor are arrested on charges of vagrancy.

For the powerful the situation is quite different. There are criminals who go unpunished because they are protected by the power of money, prestige or influence. The society that protects them becomes an accomplice to this kind of injustice. This double treatment suggests that in our society money, not people, is the source of rights.

A recent meeting of the Bar Association in Bahia gave expression to the concern of lawyers over this state of affairs. They said that penal law is the law of the poor, not because it is their guardian and protector, but because it brings to bear its force and vehemence exclusively on them.

The impunity of police criminals

The crimes of the famous Death Squad—whose operation in several States of the Federation has been confirmed—are notorious. It is publicly known that several assassins among the police were arrested and punished according to the law.

But the matter is a serious one with regard to police accused of the crimes of murder, corruption, trafficking in drugs and white slavery who are never brought to trial because high officials protect them on the allegation that they are valuable elements for the repression of political crimes.

Justice is thereby hindered from fulfilling its duty to assure the principle of equality of all people before the law which is basic to any civilized society.

Unfair land distribution

The unfair distribution of land in Brazil dates back to the colonial period. However in recent times the problem has become more acute because of the financial incentives for agribusinesses.

As a negative result, in addition to the unchecked real estate speculation going on in the interior of the country, big companies equipped with legal and financial resources do away with small operators by expelling Indians and homesteaders from their lands.

These small landholders—squatters and homesteaders—who have difficulty in getting even an identification card, cannot get title to their land or give proof in court of their right to use the land. Hence they are expelled to more remote places, even to neighbouring countries. Or they become nomads doomed to wandering the highways.

If they resist, conflicts arise of the kind which are multiplying in the Amazon and Mato Grosso regions.

Others move to nearby cities, causing a vast internal migration which is swelling urban populations. They have to live in miserable slums in a subhuman existence until they are swept farther away, as areas in which they settle are taken over for real estate speculation or for urban development. In the cities they suffer degradation from low wages. Human services for them are of miserable quality or totally lacking.

The status of Indians

Indians, especially those in the Amazonian region, are losing vast areas of land to ranchers and homesteaders—some of whom were expelled from their land by powerful companies. What is happening today is a repetition of what happened to the Indians in the southern part of the country at an earlier time.

In this framework the Indian Statute becomes a dead letter. If the Indians survive they are exploited as cheap labour, or they go to the edge of the cities, or, hungry and suffering, they wander along the highways that cut up their reservations.

The guardianship of the State, which makes them partially incompetent before the law, hinders the Indians from becoming subjects of their development and destiny. The process of surveying the Indian lands is slow. The problem is aggravated by the profits available to those who exploit mineral and forest wealth.

The introduction of a development process with vast financial backing has laid whole tribes open to extermination. This happens when highways are opened up without prior planning or respect for the first inhabitants of the area. Some INCRA (National Institute of Colonization and Agrarian Reform) projects are of this kind.

Thus it is not surprising that Indians become ashamed of their race and try to hide their origin, calling themselves Bolivians or Peruvians in order to be accepted by a society that rates itself superior.

National security and individual society

We have already said that the principle of equality of all people before the law is the foundation of any society that pretends to be civilized, and the security of each citizen is thus an essential condition for the internal security of a nation.

The Constitution now in effect affirms that all power comes from the people and is exercised in their name.

A contrary thesis maintains it is the State which grants freedom and human rights to citizens. This goes along with the principle that inspired the idea of national security, has guided the Brazilian government since 1964 and has given origin to a political system which is increasingly more centralized and with proportionally less participation by the people.

To place the State—the government—above the Nation means overvaluing state security and undervaluing individual security. This means reducing people to silence in a climate of fear.

Without the people's participation and expression the programs, projects and official plans, whatever their excellence and economic or material success, readily lead to corruption. They are not justified unless they correspond to the needs and aspirations of the people.

The ideology of national security placed above personal security is spreading throughout the Latin American continent, just as it has in countries under Soviet rule.

Inspired by this ideology military regimes claiming to fight against communism and promote economic development, have declared an anti-subversive war on all those who disagree with the authoritarian view of the organization of society.

Besides brutalizing its agents, training for such a war creates a new type of fanaticism and a climate of violence and fear. Freedom of thought and expression are sacrificed and individual guarantees are suppressed.

This doctrine has led military regimes to fall into the characteristics and practices of communist regimes: the abuse of power by the State, arbitrary arrests, tortures and suppression of freedom of thought.

Our struggle must not be against persons; they all deserve our love. Our struggle is against enslavement by sin, hunger and injustice, for which people, often unconsciously, are responsible.

Organized civil forces do not want to yield to small and weak people who are in the majority. It is only the great and powerful, who have rights. The ordinary man should have only what is strictly necessary to keep him alive to serve the powerful

It would be well for justice to punish the murderers of Fr Joao Bosco, not because he comes from an important family, but so that police agents would not be disrespectful to torture anyone—as they tortured our sisters Margarida and Santana—nor go on spreading terror among the ordinary people.

It would be well for Joao Mineiro and his partners in crime to be arrested and sentenced, not to avenge the death of Fr Rodolfo and the Indian Simao, but so that land stealers might understand that the arm of justice weighs on them, too.

Yet simple punishment of criminals cannot salve the conscience of officials as long as the socio-politico-economic system continues to create a social order which is characterized by injustice and fosters violence.' From LatinAmerica Press, December 9, 1976

11 Hollenweger, 46, pp. 81 f.

12 This estimate of the typical Pentecostal attitude towards society coincides with my own experience of Pentecostalism in Brazil (with the exception noted on p. 71), and it finds confirmation in the study of Chilean Pentecostals by d'Epinay. 'At the moment when one of the bastions of tradition is disappearing (the familial and paternalistic social system which the great land-holdings realized to the full), at that very moment the Pentecostal congregation arises which, without doubt, fills a void, by enabling the individual to be integrated into a group, organized on the old model, but at the same time making it impossible for its members to participate directly as responsible beings in the modern society which is struggling to emerge. In other words, while Pentecostalism disalienates the individual to begin with, since it allows him to overcome his uprooting and isolation by offering him entry into an organized, protective group, it then in turn alienates itself and "re-alienates" its members, since it looks upon itself as alien to the "world" and effectively makes its members strangers to society'—d'Epinay, 24, p. 130 (see his careful discussion pp. 106–45)

13 'Towards a New Aid Policy', Waldo Cesar, Cenpla, Rio de Janeiro, 1974.

14 From LatinAmerica Press, April 8, 1976

15 'I have heard the cry of my people', IDOC, Rome, 1973. For an extended quotation of this document, see Castro, 18, pp. 100–1

16 Cadernos do Centro de Estudos e Ação Social, Salvador, No. 35, Jan. 1975, p. 7

CHAPTER FOUR

1 Segundo, 40–44
2 Segundo, 73, p. 180
3 Segundo, 73, p. 181
4 Segundo, 71, p. 184
5 Cf. Costas: 'The need of the hour is not the perpetuation of para-ecclesiastical vanguard organizations, but a deeper involvement of Christians committed to the process of liberation in the regular activities of the church', 20, p. 223
6 Costas speaks of 'a naïve, uncritical attitude on the part of many Chilean Protestant leaders toward the present government ... at worst the statement and its signing represent a betrayal of the prophetic mission of the church', 20, p. 146. Moltmann is more outspoken: 'In December 1974 32 leading Protestant church officials greeted the power grab of the military junta in Chile as "God's answer to the prayers of all believers who see in Marxism a satanic power." This declaration is so atrocious that it cannot be passed over in painful silence. Whoever expects the "fulfilment of his prayers" from the terror of tyranny does not pray in the name of the crucified Messiah of the people. The God of Jesus Christ does not answer the prayers of those who believe in him through the execution of more than 10,000 poor people. With this declaration the "believers" who were referred to and their alleged "Protestant church officials" expose themselves as adherents of a murderous political religion that has nothing in common with Christianity.

'The God of the Chilean military junta is the political idol Moloch. Whoever brings his/her thank-offering to him separates him/herself from every Christian community. That is religious fascism. "Satanic powers" can only be overcome by the risen Christ, not through another satan. By declaring Marxism to be a "satanic power" one makes out of Christ an anti-communist satan. Christianity throughout the whole world will have to repent for the perverse declaration of those 32 "Protestant church officials" in Chile. It will have to turn away from such apostasy and toward new obedience', Moltmann, 63, pp. 62, 63
7 Cf. Gutierrez: 'We discover ... that the policy of non-intervention in political affairs holds for certain actions which involve ecclesiastical authorities, but not for others. In other words, this principle (that the church does not interfere in the temporal sphere) is not applied when it is a question of main-

taining the *status quo*, but it is wielded when, for example, a lay apostolic movement or a group of priests holds an attitude considered to be subversive to the established order', 45, p. 65

CHAPTER FIVE

1 Bonino, 10, xix

2 Cf. K. Grayston on 1 Cor. 4:8–13: 'Paul was writing to Christians, some of whom said that they were fulfilled, enriched and ruling. They were able to lay down the rules. Paul contrasts them with the apostles who were called on to lay down their lives' (*Expository Times*, October 1976, p. 16)

3 Gutierrez, 8 (introduction) p. 16, (my italics last sentence)

4 A number of scholars have discussed this question, including O. Cullmann, *Jesus and the Revolutionaries*, S. G. F. Brandon, *The Trial of Jesus*, and A. Richardson, *The Political Christ*. One of the best and most balanced treatments of the subject is to be found in *A Marxist looks at Jesus*, by M. Machovec, 58 (see also Hans Kung, *On Being A Christian*, Collins 1977, pp. 177 f.)

5 J. Moltmann, 61, p. 143

6 Luke 4:16 f.

7 For a careful and lucidly argued discussion of this point, cf. Davies, 25, pp. 23 f. Cf. also Gutierrez, 45, p. 230

8 Gutierrez, 45, pp. 231–2

9 Cf. Segundo, 76, p. 71. 'Whatever one may think about the political stance or the political neutrality of Jesus himself, it seems evident that his commandment of love and his countless examples and admonitions concerning it in the Gospels must be translated to an era in which real-life love has taken on political forms.'

10 Cf. R. Preston, 66, pp. 23 f.

11 One commentator, who, while expressing uneasiness, refuses to be alarmed, is D. Jenkins. His *The Contradiction of Christianity* contains one of the most balanced appraisals to date of the phenomenon, e.g. 'I believe that the Marxist diagnoses and intuitions about certain central features and forces of present social reality are the most appropriate, challenging and creative that are available to us. On the subject of obstacles to being human they have to be taken absolutely seriously. I refuse to believe however that they are to be taken absolutely, that is, as declaring and defining a total diagnosis and definition of reality. Nonetheless it is my thesis that the issue of how the

Marxist critique, challenge and programme is to be evaluated and responded to is a central critical issue in our concern for being human and becoming human, for the freedom and the future of man, and for the authenticity of Christian faith and gospel. This I hold because the Marxist critique seems to be the most powerful pointer to our sharpest present human contradictions and sources of inhumanity' 48, p. 32 (see esp. chapters 3–5)

12 Bonino, 11, p. 8

13 Sapsezian, 70, p. 259

14 See, for example, Garaudy, 36, 37; Girardi, 43; Lochman, 57; Gollwitzer, 44; Klugman and Oestreicher, 53; Gardavsky, 38; Machovec, 58

15 Preston, 66, p. 158

16 Moltmann, 63, p. 60

17 Neill, 64, p. 85. Neill both mis-quotes the title of Bonino's book, and misunderstands his criticism of Moltmann. Nowhere does Bonino imply that Moltmann in *The Crucified God* has *receded* from his earlier position in *Theology of Hope*. Indeed, Bonino specifically acknowledges Moltmann 'has brilliantly corrected and deepened his earlier insight'; his criticism is that Moltmann, acknowledging that the crucified God is a God without a country and a class, the God of the poor, oppressed and humiliated, appears to be claiming solidarity with the poor and oppressed, and yet says nothing about the *actual historical forms* in which their struggle to overcome oppression is carried forward. In fact, Bonino's criticism has now evoked from Moltmann a reply (see note 16) which indicates quite clearly that his theology does not move in an atmosphere free from ideological presupposition and specific political options, and that his own project is in the direction of social democracy. Bonino comments, 'European theologians are quite entitled to choose a social democratic analysis, ideology and programme —but they should begin by making it explicit.'

To return to Neill's treatment of Bonino. It simply will not do to suggest that Bonino's disappointment with Moltmann stems from lack of appreciation of the extent to which the reputation of the Russians has been destroyed in Europe by the violent action of the invasion of Czechoslovakia. 'Central Europe', writes Neill, 'is a long way from Latin America.' The implication that Bonino's dialogue with Marxism somehow involves condoning the foreign policy of the Soviet government is too absurd to refute; while the misplaced imputation of provincial ignorance of what goes on outside Latin America is evidence of the kind of paternalistic superiority that Latin Americans justifiably find so unacceptable. (It may not be irrelevant to add that a president of the World Council of Churches—even if Latin American—could hardly be unaware of what is going on outside his own country!)

18 Segundo, 76, p. 108
19 Bonino, 11, p. 21
20 Torres, 40, pp. 261 f.
21 Alves, 4, p. 16
22 'What would Thomas Aquinas do about Karl Marx?'— *Sisyphus Papers*, April 1975, Office of Social Ministries Jesuit Conference, quoted in LatinAmerica Press, December 4, 1975
23 Sanders, *Christianity and Crisis*, September 17, 1973, pp. 167 f.
24 Preston, 66, pp. 159 f.
25 Hebblethwaite. 'How liberating is liberation theology?', *Frontier*, Winter 1975/6, p. 202. Cf. Don Cupitt in *The Listener*, July 29, 76: 'The Bible is about a people's education. They learnt that the state is not divine, and no political cause is sacred. Political and religious obligation are distinct, and not to be confused. All political authority, and all political aspirations, are under divine judgement. Ever since, there has been a distinction between religion and politics which has set the prophet against the king, the Baptist and Jesus against Herod and Pilate, the church against the state. Christianity has never had a doctrine of a holy war, and cannot simply identify political liberation with religious salvation.'
26 Gutierrez, 45, p. 234
27 Ch. 1, pp. 33 f.
28 Alves, 6, pp. 173–6
29 Gutierrez, 45, pp. 232–9
30 Cf. de Santa Ana, 68, p. 190
31 Bonino, 10, p. 149
32 Bonino, 10, p. 87
33 Cf. Jenkins, 48, pp. 7 f., for an honest admission of what he calls the 'tribalism' of white bourgeois theology
34 Cf. Moltmann, 61, p. 323; Alves, 6, *passim*
35 Assmann, 8, p. 60
36 Segundo's discussion of the relation between faith and ideology is one of the most comprehensive and closely argued available. He devotes three chapters to the problem. But his analysis of

the unsuccessful attempt of the Chilean bishops to avoid an ideological stance during the Allende period is so relevant here that it deserves quoting in full.

'During the first year of Allende's presidency, when many of the disturbing factors that would later show up had not yet appeared on the scene, the bishops issued a draft document entitled *Evangelio, politica y socialismos* ("The Gospel Message, Politics, and Brands of Socialism"). Here I cannot give a full-length summary of that document, which is a history-making document in the relationship between faith and ideologies in the Latin American Church. But I do want to point up one important and curious fact which seems to have eluded the attention of the document's authors: on the one hand the document asserts that the Church cannot opt or choose sides, on the other hand it says that in Chile socialism is not a real alternative to the existing capitalist system. The explanation for this curious contradiction has a great deal to do with the relationship between faith and ideologies.

Why cannot the Church choose sides? According to the Chilean bishops, it cannot do that because in practice it would mean excluding from the Church that portion of Christians who had opted for the other side. But in their view the Church belongs to all the people of Chile. In other words, to use our terminology, it means that the one faith must not be put in the service of ideologies, which are many and varied by very definition.

This is a very important point because it contains some critical underlying assumptions. Firstly, it is an admission that ideologies are in fact more appealing than the faith to the Christian people, even though they should not be. Indeed they are so appealing that they would separate a good portion of the faithful from the *practice* of the faith at least. Thus on the one hand the bishops are stating what ought to be: the faith that unites us is more important than the ideologies that divide us. On the other hand they are admitting that this is not the real-life feeling and disposition of Christians. Secondly, it presupposes a theological conception of the faith in which faith itself is the most important thing, quite aside from any and all ideological options one may make out of fidelity to that faith. But we are quite justified in asking: Why is it more important? I do not think any answer to that question can be found in the guidelines laid down by Vatican II, which suggest that the function of faith is to lead the human mind to fully human solutions. The implications of those guidelines are that the importance of the faith lies precisely in its connection with the different and even opposed solutions that are offered for our problems in history. So we have every right to assume that the Chilean bishops, despite the guidelines of Vatican II, continue to picture the faith as a direct means of eternal salvation whereas ideologies are seen as merely human options that can jeopardize that other superior value.

But as I suggested earlier, the most noteworthy and important point seems to be that the bishops, who claim they cannot choose sides, come out and say that socialism cannot be an alternative to the existing capitalist system, as things now stand in Chile. We are perfectly justified in asking: By what curious mental process did the bishops convince themselves that they were not choosing sides when they made that statement?

Remember that the Chilean bishops start out maintaining that it is not possible for the Church to choose between *ideologies*. It does not occur to them to deny that the *faith* is an option. What they say is that the option of faith should be divested of any and every element which is not the faith itself. In other words, no ideological option should condition the option of faith in any way. But right after they have said that the Church cannot opt for one (ideological) group against another, they go on to say: 'The Church opts for the risen Christ.' In the context it might sound a little odd, but actually it makes perfect sense in terms of their conception of faith. In their eyes, opting for the risen Christ comes down to making one possible option between the nooks and crannies of any and every ideology.

But how is it that the bishops end up opting for the capitalist ideology as opposed to the socialist ideology? The answer is obvious enough. In saying that socialism is not an acceptable alternative to the existing capitalist system, the bishops are not at all aware of the fact that they are choosing between ideologies. Strange as it may seem to us, they think that they are avoiding an ideological option in saying that.

The mental process at work here is clear enough. In the eyes of the bishops, the existing reality is not an ideology; it is simply reality. They have no doubt that it should be corrected but, as they see it, reality as such does not splinter the faith. So long as no ideologies about this *reality* arise, faith has nothing to fear from the *fact* that extremely wealthy human beings live alongside extremely poor human beings. The problem arises when an *ideology* challenges this *reality*. The great sin of "Christians for Socialism" in other words, is that there is no party of "Christians for Capitalism". Of course such people exist, but they do not have to join together under a banner to exercise their influence and carry out their program. But any attempt to put through a radical change in the existing structures must present itself as an *ideology*. It must knock on the door of the Christian heart and appeal to its relationship with the authentic values of the faith.

We must understand the language of the Chilean bishops in order to understand and appreciate their mentality and their theology. In saying that socialism is not a proper alternative to capitalism, they are not saying that socialist Christians are heretics. They are perfectly capable of remaining Christians in spite of their mistake, because it is a practical not a dogmatic mistake. But they should admit that the existing reality is sufficient for the faith. If they do not admit that, then they are relativizing the faith by imposing a condition on it: i.e., that the existing structures be changed, that people accept an ideology proposing such change. The episcopal document summons Christians to maintain a certain brand of prudent reserve. They must recognize the fact that the really important and decisive thing, faith, is possible in any and every set of circumstances. And since it is the decisive thing, it cannot be subordinated to those circumstances and their attendant ideologies.

That this is the great sin of an ideology is evident from the way in which the Chilean bishops analyze the *socialist* ideology. The various steps in their analysis are quite clear. Firstly, in any journey towards socialism Christians will be in a minority and the socialist ideology must be given its proper label: i.e. *Marxist*. The second step is to take the feature of Marxism which seems to be most directly connected with the Christian faith—that is, *atheism*—and link it up with all the historical defects and dehumanizing elements that are evident in those societies where Marxism has triumphed so far. It does not seem to strike the bishops that they have often denounced the same dehumanizing elements in capitalist society without making any reference to its atheism or its religiosity. And it is worth noting that the elements overlooked in their analysis are precisely those elements which link up faith with ideologies' *Liberation of Theology*, pp. 130–3. It is worth comparing this with David Jenkins' comments on the ideological conflict in Britain in the early months of 1974 (48, p. 35)

37 Batson, 9, p. 12

38 Batson, 9, p. 188

39 In fact, Segundo's exposition of the relation between faith and ideology seems to come fairly close, at the end, to what Batson *et al* are saying. 'Faith without works is dead. Faith without ideologies is equally dead. Faith incarnated in successive ideologies constitutes an ongoing educational process in which man learns how to learn under God's guidance. We will never be able to reduce the faith to a specific book or page of the Bible, to a specific Creed, or to a specific dogma. All of these things point out the *road to be travelled* by faith, but they never provide us with the journey completed' *Liberation of Theology*, p. 181. Cf. Batson *et al*: 'The Christian is challenged by Jesus to be committed to growth in a particular direction, outward towards others; and, moreover, to expression of this growth in responsible action' *Commitment without Ideology*, p. 12

40 A point reported by Dr Ian Fraser in *Cuba Now: Signs of the Kingdom*, Movement Pamphlet, 1976, p. 12. C. F. Wren, 80, pp. 103–14

41 Quoted in *Financial Times*, 26 November 1976

42 *Cuba Now: Signs of the Kingdom*, p. 5

43 Quoted in Bonino, 10, p. 42

44 Torres, 40, pp. 289–90

45 Bonino, 11, p. 129. Cf. Jenkins, 48, p. 69: 'Unless sinfulness is recognized as something shared in by all human beings, then there is no escape from the dehumanizing limitations of false and premature absolutes proclaimed by limited and partial agents of a partially understood historical process.'

46 Cf. Bonino, 10, p. 87

47 Freire, 32, pp. 46 f.

48 ISEDET report for 1974, Buenos Aires

49 Bonino, 10, xix

50 Gutierrez, 45, p. 308

51 Freire, 33, pp. 51 f.

52 See *Curso Nueva Vida en Cristo*, No. 8, 'Pueblo Nuevo; Mundo Nuevo'

53 *International Review of Mission*, Vol. LXIV, No. 254 April 1975

54 IDOC, Rome, 'The Future of the Missionary Enterprise'

55 A point made by A. Sapsezian in a taped interview, part of 'Latin America', a study pack published by MMS/USPG

56 Cf. the extraordinarily vivid accounts of life in Latin American slums, Lewis, 56, and Carolina Maria de Jesus, 49
57 Cf. Davies, 25, pp. 130 f.
58 Camara, 17, p. 12
59 *The Observer*, 12 September 1976
60 Klugman, 77, pp. 49 f.
61 Garaudy, 37, p. 207

FOR FURTHER READING

NOTE: The bulk of Latin American theology of liberation is, of course, written in Spanish and Portuguese. I have deliberately confined this bibliography to books and articles in English, most of them readily accessible to the English reader. A selection of books of wider theological and political relevance is also included in the list.

1 AGEE, P. *Inside the Company: CIA Diary*, Penguin 1975
2 ALVES, Rubem A. *A Theology of Human Hope*, World Publishing Co. 1969, Abbey Press 1975
3 ——. *Tomorrow's Child*, SCM 1972
4 ——. Marxism as the Guarantee of Faith, *Worldview*, March 1973, pp. 13–17
5 ——. Confessions: On Theology and Life, *Union Seminary Quarterly Review*, Vol. XXIX, Nos. 3 and 4, Spring and Summer 1974
6 ——. Christian Realism: Ideology of the Establishment, *Christianity and Crisis*, September 17, 1973, pp. 173 f.
7 ——. The Crisis in the Congregation, *International Review of Mission*, Vol. LX, No. 237, January 1971
8 ASSMANN, H. *Theology for a Nomad Church*. Orbis Books (published as *Practical Theology of Liberation*, Search Press 1975)
9 BATSON, C. D. *et al. Commitment without Ideology*, SCM 1973
10 BONINO, José Miguez. *Doing Theology in a Revolutionary Situation*, Fortress Press 1975 (published as *Revolutionary Theology Comes of Age*, SPCK 1975)
11. ——. *Christians and Marxists: The Mutual Challenge to Revolution*, Hodder and Stoughton 1976
12 ——. Our Debt as Evangelicals to the Roman Catholic Community, *Ecumenical Review*, Vol. XXI, No. 4, October 1969
13 ——. Five Theses on Theology of Liberation, *Expository Times*, April 1976
14 BRUNEAU, T. *The Political Transformation of the Brazilian Catholic Church*, C.U.P. 1974

15 CAMARA, Helder. *Church and Colonialism*, Sheed and Ward 1969
16 ——. *Race Against Time*, Sheed and Ward
17 ——. *Spiral of Violence*, Sheed and Ward 1971
18 CASTRO, Emilio. *Amidst Revolution*, Christian Journals Ltd 1975
19 COSTAS, Orlando E. *The Church and its Mission: A Shattering Critique from the Third World*, Tyndale Ho. Publishers 1974
20 ——. *Theology of the Crossroads in Latin America*, Rodopi 1976
21 COX, Harvey. *The Seduction of the Spirit: The Use and Misuse of People's Religion*, Wildwood House 1974
22 d'ANTONIO, W. V. and PIKE, F. B. (eds.). *Religion, Revolution and Reform*, Burns and Oates 1965
23 de BROUCKER, JOSE. *Dom Helder Camara: The Violence of a Peacemaker*, Orbis Books 1970
24 d'EPINAY, C. L. *Haven of the Masses: A study of the Pentecostal Movement in Chile*, Lutterworth Press 1969
25 DAVIES, J. G. *Christians, Politics and Violent Revolution*, SCM 1976
26 DEBRAY, R. *Che's Guerrilla War*, Penguin 1975
27 ——. *Prison Writings*, Penguin 1975
28 DUSSEL. *History and the Theology of Liberation*, Orbis Books 1976
29 EAGLESON, J. (ed.). *Christians and Socialism: Documentation of the Christians for Socialism Movement in Latin America*, Orbis Books 1975
30 EAGLESON, J. and GARCIA, E. (eds.). *My Life for My Friends: the Guerrilla Journal of Nestor Paz, Christian*, Orbis Books 1975
31 ELLIOTT, C. *The Development Debate*, SCM 1971
32 FREIRE, P. *The Pedagogy of the Oppressed*, Penguin 1972
33 ——. *Cultural Action for Freedom*, Penguin 1972
34 FRASER, Ian. *The Fire Runs*, SCM 1974
35 GALLET, P. *Freedom to Starve*, Penguin 1972
36 GARAUDY, R. *From Anathema to Dialogue*, Collins 1967
37 ——. *The Alternative Future: a Vision of Christian Marxism*, Penguin 1976
38 GARDAVSKI, V. *God is Not Yet Dead*, Penguin 1973
39 GERASSI, J. *The Great Fear*, Macmillan, New York, 1963
40 GERASSI, J. (ed.). *Revolutionary Priest: The Complete Writings and Messages of Camilo Torres*, Random House 1971

41 GERASSI, J. (ed.). *Venceremos! The Speeches and Writings of Che Guevara*, Panther Books 1969
42 GHEERBRANT, A. *The Rebel Church in Latin America*, Penguin 1974
43 GIRARDI, G. *Marxism and Christianity*, MacMillan 1968
44 GOLLWITZER, H. *Christian Faith and the Marxist Criticism of Religion*, St Andrews Press 1970
45 GUTIERREZ, G. *A Theology of Liberation*, Orbis Books 1973, SCM 1974
46 HOLLENWEGER, W. J. *Pentecost Between Black and White*, Christian Journals Ltd 1974
47 ILLICH, Ivan. *Celebration of Awareness: a call for Institutional Revolution*, Penguin 1973
48 JENKINS, D. *The Contradiction of Christianity*, SCM 1976
49 JESUS, Carolina Maria de. *Beyond All Pity*, Panther 1973
50 JULIAO, Francisco. *Cambao: The Yoke*, Penguin 1972
51 KADT, E. *Catholic Radicals in Brazil*, O.V.P. 1970
52 KEE, A. *A Reader in Political Theology*, SCM 1974
53 KLUGMAN, J. and OESTREICHER, P. (eds.). *What Kind of Revolution?* Panther 1968
54 LEHMANN, P. *Ethics in a Christian Context*, Harper and Row 1963
55 ——. *The Transfiguration of Politics: Jesus Christ and the Question of Revolution*, SCM 1975
56 LEWIS, O. *The Children of Sanchez*, Penguin 1964
57 LOCHMAN, J. *Encountering Marx*, Christian Journals Ltd 1977
58 MACHOVEC, M. *A Marxist looks at Jesus*, Darton, Longman and Todd 1976
59 MIRANDA, J. *Marx and the Bible*, Orbis Books 1974, SCM 1976
60 MOLTMANN, J. *Theology of Hope*, SCM 1967
61 ——. *The Crucified God*, SCM 1974
62 ——. *The Experiment Hope*, SCM 1975
63 ——. An Open Letter to José Miguez Bonino, *Christianity and Crisis*, March 29, 1976, pp. 67–73
64 NEILL, S. *Salvation Tomorrow*, Lutterworth 1976
65 Peruvian Bishops Commission for Social Action. *Between Honesty and Hope*, Orbis Books 1970
66 PRESTON, R. H. (ed.). *Theology and Change: Essays in Memory of Alan Richardson*, SCM 1975
67 ROBERTSON, E. H. *Tomorrow is a Holiday*, SCM 1959
68 SANTA ANA, Julio de. The Influence of Bonhoeffer on the Theology of Liberation, *The Ecumenical Review*, Vol. XXVIII, No. 2, April 1976

69 SAPSEZIAN, A. In Search of a Grass-roots Ministry, *International Review of Mission*, Vol. LX, No. 238, April 1971

70 ——. Theology of Liberation—Liberation of Theology: Educational Perspectives, *Theological Education*, Vol. IX, No. 4, Summer 1973

71 SEGUNDO, J. L. *The Community Called Church*, Orbis Books 1973

72 ——. *Grace and the Human Condition*, Orbis Books 1973

73 ——. *Our Idea of God*, Orbis Books 1974

74 ——. *The Sacraments Today*, Orbis Books 1974

75 ——. *Evolution and Guilt*, Orbis Books 1974

76 ——. *The Liberation of Theology*, Orbis Books 1976

77. Theological Collections, No. 13 (Klugmann, J., Pannenberg, W., *et al.*), SPCK 1970

78 VELIZ, C. (ed.). *Obstacles to Change in Latin America*, O.U.P. 1965

79 WEBB, Pauline. *Salvation Today*, S.C.M. 1974

80 WREN, Brian. *Education for Justice*, S.C.M. 1977